Venable Herndon writes screenplays ('Alice's Restaurant', with Arthur Penn) and plays ('Until the Monkey Comes'). He went to Princeton and Harvard, worked on Madison Avenue and was a founder of *Chelsea Review*. He lives in New York with poet Honor Moore who took some of the photographs for this book.

To Adeline Nall, who first recognised James Dean as an artist.

Venable Herndon

James Dean

A Short Life

Futura Publications Limited

A Futura Book

First published in Great Britain in 1974
by Futura Publications Limited

This edition published in 1974
Copyright © Venable Herndon 1974

Grateful acknowledgment is given for permission to
reprint the following: Lines from 'Rebel Without a Cause'
and 'Giant', publicity material for 'East of Eden', 'Giant'
and 'Rebel Without a Cause', and several photographs.
Reprinted by permission of Warner Bros.

ISBN 0 8600 7171 5
Printed in Great Britain by
Hazell Watson & Viney Ltd
Aylesbury, Bucks

Futura Publications Limited
49 Poland Street,
London WIA 2LG

ACKNOWLEDGMENTS

There are a number of people to whom I am especially indebted.

Adeline Nall was kind enough to let me have the use of her seventeen-year collection of James Dean material. She also graciously made herself available for long hours of conversation in which she offered invaluable insights into the life and character of her former pupil.

Donald Bogle decided that this book should exist and stuck with it through all the stages of its development.

Betty Prashker offered support and guidance, and the opportunity to satisfy criteria informed by extraordinary intelligence.

Diane Matthews gave exact and exacting criticism together with help and encouragement.

Carla Lennox found the hard-to-find photographs.

Joel Zucker, busy with a thesis on Kazan, was generous enough to share the James Dean information he discovered along his own research route.

Jay Sanford and Susan Nerenberg stayed in my corner when it counted most.

Acknowledgments

John Walton's healing hands gave me the strength to stay on the job.

George Papanek helped me construct a sanctuary safe from inner and outer monsters.

Emily Levine, a writer-entertainer, who also types, brought two drafts out of a forest of hand-written corrections, and never grew too weary to offer the full truth of her heart and mind.

Honor Moore shared her life with me and the book, pointed out flaws, demanded detail, gave praise untarnished by competitiveness, all while running a poetry series, writing poetry, and suffering the death of her mother.

And I want to thank Ben Alcock, Patsy D'Amore, Steve Aronson, Jim Backus, John Beck, Jeff Berg, Lew Bracker, Frances Britton, Joe Brown, Philip Carlson, Marvin Carter, Stockard Channing, Martin Chavez, Dick Clayton, Erin Clermont, Jonathan Coppelman, Robert Cushman, Severn Darden, Dick Davalos, Alex Dearborn, Samson DeBrier, Marion Dougherty, Richard Dunlap, Mildred Dunnock, Rudi Fehr, Sue Foster, Barbara and Jerry Garner, Bob Garon, Ruth Goetz, Jim Grindle, Julie Harris, Bill Haworth, Maggie Henderson, Otie Hunter, Kurt Kasznar, Elia Kazan, Laurie Kennedy, Lyle Kessler, Laurie Kohn, Marty Landau, Jack Larsen, Dick Lederer, Joe Lesueur, Bob Levine, Kathleen Litterie, Arthur Loew Jr., Peter Maloney, Paul Mazursky, Monica McCall, Sal Mineo, Patricia Motal, Paul Moreno, Paul Morrissey, Tye Morrow, Ronald Nelson, Maila Nurmi, Paul Osborne, John O'Steen, Gene Owen, Marvin Paige, Eugenia Paterson, Jerry Payne, George Platt, Judy Polansky, Nikos Pscharopolous, Robert Pulley, Fred Prail, Tony Ray,

Acknowledgments

Lenny Rosenman, Harrold Rust, Geoff Sanford, Paul Schmidt, Ray Schmidt, Rob Sickinger, Charles Silver, Stewart Stern, George Stevens, Juliet Taylor, Eleanor Timberman, Eli Tulman, Kathryn Walker, Paul Weaver, Sam Weill, Adrienne Welles, James Whitmore, Andrew Winner, Marcus and Ortense Winslow, Jane Withers, Peter Witt.

FOREWORD

On September 30, 1972, the seventeenth anniversary of James Dean's death in a California car crash, photographer Honor Moore and I drove to a small cemetery just north of the farming town of Fairmount, Indiana, and took up watch near the dead star's grave. Jimmy's aunt and uncle, Ortense and Marcus Winslow, had told us that even after all these years people came to the grave on his birthday and on this, his deathday.

It took about half an hour to find the medium-sized pinkish granite stone (JAMES B. DEAN 1931–1955) on top of a slight rise, facing west. We stopped our big boat of a rented car in one of the cemetery's narrow gravel alleys and waited.

For a long while nothing happened. An occasional pickup, several cars, and a tractor passed on the road that runs alongside the cemetery. Nobody turned in. We were beginning to think that Jimmy's fans had finally forsaken him when an old black sedan came through the gate, drove directly to the grave, and stopped. An old man in a dark overcoat and workingman's cap got out. He looked in our direction for a moment, walked over to the gravestone, stared at it without particular curiosity, walked back to his car, stood beside it. From time to time he glanced at the cemetery gate. He was waiting for people, too.

Twenty minutes went by. The sun slipped further down the sky, and although there was no wind, the air got noticeably colder. Suddenly an orange Volkswagen popped over the hill and pulled up beside the grave. Three young men climbed out. One had on a bright red nylon jacket, and blue pants, and his unruly blond hair was brushed straight back off a high forehead. For just a moment, until we could see that the hair was dyed, and that the face was not precisely Jimmy's, it looked as though James Dean was standing beside his own grave. Honor and I looked at each other and shivered. One of the fake Jimmy's companions put a basket of flowers down beside the gravestone where other flowers, plastic and real, were already weathering.

The old man in the workingman's cap walked over to the three young men and began a conversation which we were too far away to overhear. The old man paid no special attention to Jimmy's double. The three young men did not smile. They were interested in what the old man was saying, but it was evident that his presence had profaned what was to have been a sacred, silent moment at the grave. Soon they got back into the orange Volkswagen and drove away, passing near enough to let us see that they had an Illinois license plate.

We expected the old man to take up his station beside the black sedan again, but instead, he signaled us to come over to him at the grave. Closer up he looked like a slightly more robust André Gide: black-framed glasses, brimmed cap substituting for Basque beret, bright, intelligent eyes. He said his name was Bing Traster, and that he was a landscape gardener in Fairmount, where he had known Jimmy Dean as a boy. He said he came to the grave on Jimmy's birthdays and deathdays to talk to visitors, and tell them his stories: Jimmy and his schoolmates hanging around the tree nursery to cadge forbidden cigarettes from hired hands, Jimmy roaring down Main Street on his first motorcycle, Jimmy listening to stories about his father, Winton, whom Bing had also known as a young man.

Then Bing announced that he was a champion liar and pulled out a newspaper clipping showing (there he was in the picture) that he had indeed won a state lying contest three years earlier in Bloomington, Indiana. We looked surprised, even upset. He understood. Quickly he reassured us that he had been telling the absolute truth about Jimmy. After all, didn't it take a good liar to know what was true? He glanced at the sun, now almost on the horizon. He decided to call it a day, got back into the black sedan, gave us the barest hint of a smile, and drove off.

We stood near the grave for a few more minutes, trying to shake off the feeling that we were in a dream. It was good to hear the car engine start, and we were glad to get back to a warm motel room in the world of the living.

15

In the weeks and months that followed that visit to the graveyard I tracked back over James Dean's life, town by town, city by city, TV part by TV part, play by play, movie by movie. I talked to Jimmy's relatives, his schoolmates, his teachers, his co-stars, his directors, his lovers, his friends, his enemies. I drove and flew thousands of miles, ran up enormous phone bills, made dozens of tapes, read millions of words, looked at hundreds of photographs, saw James Dean's movies over and over again. And because James Dean was born an Aquarius on the threshold of the Aquarian age, I commissioned John Beck, an astrologer who knew nothing of Dean's life, to do his chart. By the time Beck had finished his work, the bulk of my interviewing and researching and writing was complete. It was amazing to see that so many of the secrets I had discovered on earth were also to be found in the stars (see Appendix).

James Dean left his uncle's Indiana farm in 1949, when he was eighteen years old. Five years later he was a famous film star. Then, in the fall of 1955, when he was only twenty-four, he died at the wheel of his Porsche Spyder. His death touched off a film-fan frenzy that rivaled the explosion of feeling that followed the death of Rudolph Valentino. In the years after the fatal crash Warner Brothers got as many as seven thousand letters a month addressed to a James Dean whose absence from earth fans simply refused to accept. Only last year sensation sheets like the *National Examiner* were hawking copies with the headline: "JAMES DEAN DID NOT DIE IN

'FATAL' AUTO ACCIDENT. PARALYZED AND MUTILATED, HE'S HIDDEN IN A SANATORIUM."

On screen (in his three films: *East of Eden, Rebel Without a Cause, Giant*) and in life James Dean acted out the restlessness and rebellion that youth in the status quo fifties felt but could not express. His passionate and futile confrontations with authority stirred shock waves of empathy in millions of people who sensed that there was something rotten under the arrogant apathy of the Eisenhower era, something unnamably ominous about the McCarthy-Nixon inquisition.

It was only for the middle-class, middle-aged white men who traditionally dominate American society that James Dean's rebellion was *without* a cause. For kids, for women, for blacks, the cause was real even though it had not yet flamed into the on-the-street struggle for the eighteen-year-old vote, for liberation, for civil rights, that was to sear through the sixties.

James Dean was well on his way to being a mythic hero while he was alive. His death completed the consecration, assuring him a place in a pantheon that includes other wounded, gifted people who felt life too intensely to bear living it: Arthur Rimbaud, Charles Baudelaire, Lenny Bruce, Billie Holiday, Charlie Parker, Dylan Thomas, Jackson Pollock, Sylvia Plath, Janis Joplin, Jimi Hendrix.

But the trouble with myth is that it often conceals rather than reveals the true nature of the hero or heroine. As the years have passed the image of James Dean the dragon killer, the David who took on Goliath, the Icarus whose wings were singed off by the sun, has grown clearer

17

and clearer. The image of James Dean the person had grown dim.

Out of two years of searching and thinking and writing comes a portrait of the person, a boy becoming a man, sometimes in sharp conflict with his myth, sometimes indistinguishable from it.

And beyond the private person and the star-hero there was another Dean, the actor, in whom both other figures combined. It is Dean's achievements as an actor that inspired me to set out in search of him, and my curiosity about a person who could wage, and even for a little while win, the battle of Hollywood.

ONE

"I, James Byron Dean was born February 8, 1931, Marion, Indiana, My parents, Winton Dean and Mildred Dean formerly Mildred Wilson, and myself existed in the state of Indiana until I was six years of age.

"Dad's work with the government caused a change so Dad as a dental mechanic was transferred to California. There we lived until the fourth year. Mom became ill and passed out of my life at the age of nine. I never knew the reason for Mom's death, in fact it still preys on my mind.

"I had always lived such a talented life. I studied violin, played in concerts, tap-danced on theatre stages but most of all I like art, to mold and create things with my hands.

"I came back to Indiana to live with my uncle. I lost the dancing and violin but not the art. I think my life will be devoted to art and dramatics. And there are so many different fields of art it would be hard to foul up, and if I did there are so many different things to do—farm, sports, science, geology, coaching, teaching, music. I got it and I know if I better myself that there will be no match. A fellow must have confidence.

"When living in California my young eyes experienced many things. It was also my luck to make three visiting trips to Indiana, going and coming a different route each time. I have been in almost every state west of Indiana. I remember all.

"My hobby, or what I do in my spare time, is motorcycle. I know a lot about them mechanically and I love to ride. I have been in a few races and I have done well. I own a small cycle myself. When I'm not doing that I'm usually engaged in athletics, the heart beat of every American boy. As one strives to make a goal in a game there should be a goal in this crazy world for each of us. I hope I know where mine is, anyway, I'm after it.

"I don't mind telling you, Mr. Dubois, this is the hardest subject to write about considering the information one knows of himself, I ever attempted."

Jimmy wrote this prophetic piece, which he called *My Case Study*, in the fall of 1948, when he was a seventeen-year-old high school senior in Fairmount, Indiana. The new principal, Roland Dubois, had been brought in from another school and had asked his students to write short autobiographies so he could get to know them. If he had called on Jimmy to read his composition aloud he would have heard him pronounce motorcycle, "motor*sickle*." Bike buffs in Fairmount still say it that way.

But Jimmy isn't born to country talk. As his "case study" tells us, his birthplace is Marion, Indiana, a city (about 50,000 in the 1930 census) ten miles north of rural Fairmount. And even in the thirties Marion is more than a whistle stop. It is served by the Chicago, Cincinnati & Louisville, the Cleveland, Cincinnati, Chicago & St. Louis, the Toledo, St. Louis & Western and by electrified lines from nearby Indianapolis, Muncie, Kokomo, Wabash, Peru, and a long timetable of smaller manufacturing and farming centers on Indiana's broad Till plain.

Marion makes stoves and iron bedsteads, blows glass, forges foundry tools, processes paper pulp, tans hides, was once an important supplier of natural gas: after the Civil War a senator from the Hoosier State talked Washington into building an Old Soldiers' Home in Marion by arguing that an eternal supply of natural gas—"free light and heat for our brave boys!"—went right along with the real estate. About 1906, the "eternal" gas gave out. But the old soldiers stayed on, and after the First World War their "home" began to be called a Veterans Administration Hospital.

In 1930, Winton Dean completes his training in Chicago and gets a job at the hospital as a dental technician. He is one of the fortunate few. The big depression is on. All around Marion there are fields of rich calcareous loam. They can produce an abundance of corn, wheat, hay, oats, rye, potatoes, apples, pears. They can support large dairy herds. But right now there is little money for seed or feed. People in Grant County are just managing to eat and keep warm. Nevertheless, Winton, and his bride of one year, Mildred (daughter of John Wilson, a stocky iron worker from Gas City), manage with a regular government pay check to lead almost normal lives. In the face of the plummeting national birth rate, they are expecting a baby.

By eleven o'clock on the night of February 7, 1931, twenty-one-year-old Mildred is in labor. Winton calls the family physician. Shortly after midnight, the doctor arrives at the house, the back half of a tall, sharp-roofed clapboard structure known as "The Seven Gables," on the corner of South McClure and East Fourth Street. At two o'clock in the morning, February 8, Mildred gives birth. It's a boy.

The Deans name their son James Byron: James after James Amick, a dentist at the VA hospital whom Winton admires, and Byron after Byron Vice, one of Winton's friends.

Hollywood legend now has it that Jimmy's artistically gifted mother (she played the piano) named him after Lord Byron. That may have been one of the reasons why Mildred liked the name, but no one in the family remembers any mention of the poet at the time of the baby's naming. (Jimmy will not be baptized because the Quaker sect to which the Deans belong does not believe in christening.)

While baby Jimmy is flailing about in what is just then being introduced as a "bathinette," another Quaker, Herbert Hoover, is awash in the White House. By October 1931, bank failures have soared to the awful total of 2,342. Overnight, the Greek temples on Main Street have turned into shoeshine parlors and fruit stands, an *Alice in Wonderland* transformation that is bizarre and terrifying.

There is no Federal Deposit Insurance Corporation to make the spectacle any less awful.

In the same month, with the help of the other, even more frightening, Hoover, J. Edgar, the FBI, wielding its newest-fangled gimmick—indictment for income tax evasion, finally nabs Prohibition's most untouchable Untouchable, Chicago's own Al Capone. His fine is a piddling fifty grand, but his sentence is eleven long years in the pen. While he rots of syphilis at Alcatraz, his underlings go right on building a better Mafia.

In spite of the terrible times, richies on the right and grafters on the left troupe down to Washington bearing locality-booming presents for the President. The good Mr. Hoover takes time out from his business-as-usual business to allow the "newspaper boys" to snap pictures of him posing with Long Island oysters, Boston cod, Iowa bulls. Unfortunately, the well-fed smiles he flashes across these gourmet raw materials do little to reassure the people standing in bread lines or cheer the defeated men riding the rods. Thousands of people are sleeping in box cars and crouching around fires in hobo jungles where they are sometimes maimed or murdered by company bulls or marauding vigilantes. Lynching, a more ritualized form of sacrifice, also provides relief. There is a lynching in Marion in 1930 or 1931. Amos 'n' Andy don't josh about things like that on the air, of course. They are both white.

At the age of four months, Baby Jimmy is sitting up in a bright white smock, smiling puckishly into the lens of Daddy's camera.

On Inauguration Day 1933, in the open back of a

chauffeured Cadillac, Herbert Hoover rides out of office and Franklin Delano Roosevelt rides in. Things have gotten so bad by now that even the New York *Daily News* pledges (on March 6, 1933) "to support the policies of President Franklin D. Roosevelt for a period of at least one year from today; longer, if circumstances warrant." Further on, the editorial confesses that "it is no small sacrifice for a newspaper to make the pledge that is made above."

Jimmy is two, and he stands in white short-sleeved blouse, white shorts, white socks, white shoes, beside his Aunt Ortense (Winton's older sister) and his cousin Joan (Aunt Ortense's daughter) for a sun-drenched photo in front of the big white barn on Uncle Marcus' farm.

Jimmy is almost three. Winton and Mildred go about their lives quietly, uncomplainingly, relatively safe at the center of the economic storm. Winton works hard on inlays and bridges. Mildred cooks and cleans and takes care of little Jimmy Byron, as she is fond of calling him.

The world outside, when it does enter their lives, comes in through the speaker of the radio. In the afternoons, there are organ-floated soap operas: *"Road of Life," "Our Gal Sunday," "One Man's Family,"* sagas in which age-old psychological dilemmas divert the mind from the social evils of the present. At night one can try to laugh with Colonel Lemuel Q. Stoopnagle and Budd, or take a sarcastic stroll down Allen's Alley, with Fred, his wife Portland, and their friends: Senator Claghorn, Titus Moody, Mrs. Nussbaum, et. al. (That Allen did not find everything as funny as he made it sound became clear later in his savagely titled autobiography, *Treadmill to Oblivion.*)

At three, Jimmy poses for a snapshot in the Dean sitting room. His linen is freshly starched and pressed as always. His short-sleeved sailor shirt bears a big blue star on each wing of its wide collar and both port and starboard suspenders sport a shiny metal anchor. On both sides of an arrow-straight part not quite in the center of his large head Mildred has brushed the hair flat toward his prominent ears. His eyes shine with reflected affection.

Jimmy is a precocious kid. He learns to talk early. He learns to walk early. Early too, Mildred and Winton become aware of a ferocious obstinacy in their child. The boy has a will of his own. "You'd try," recalls Winton, "to order him to do or not to do something and he'd just sit there with his little face all screwed up and closed. It didn't take you very long to realize that you weren't going to get anywhere with him. Spankings didn't help. Scolding didn't. And you couldn't bribe him. But you could always reason with him, or appeal to his better instincts. He was that way even when he grew to manhood."

On weekends, Winton and Mildred often take Jimmy out to Aunt Ortense and Uncle Marcus' farm near Fairmount. Jimmy is allowed to sit at table for the big Sunday dinner. Afterward, he is sent out to play with Cousin Joan. She is five years older. She gets very bored with "the baby." Jimmy longs for the day when he will be old enough to explore the big farm all by himself.

When the Deans don't go to the Winslows, they visit Jimmy's paternal grandparents in Fairmount. Charles and

Emma Woolen Dean live in a white clapboard house on Washington Street. The family has been in Grant County since about 1815, when some Deans came out from Lexington, Kentucky, moving west for better land as so many of their neighbors had already done. They are farmers and auctioneers. Grandpa Dean is always busy with something, buying and selling cows and horses, auctioning off houses and farms, running a livery stable, selling automobiles, racing a string of ponies. Jimmy adores him. Charlie often puts his grandson on his knee and pretends to auction him off. Grandma keeps raising the bid until Grandpa shouts, "Sold to the highest bidder," and hands him over to Grandma. Everybody laughs.

The Deans are known for their love of fun, their practical jokes, their wit. One day, long after Jimmy's death, when Charlie Dean had gotten too old to walk without a cane and almost too old to drive, his car stalled out dead across a railroad track. He could see the train coming straight at him and had just time enough to get out before the locomotive struck. Down the street at his two pump filling station, Jerry Payne heard a piercing screech of metal against metal. He ran toward the crossing. There he found old Charlie Dean, leaning on his cane, holding up a seat cushion, muttering, "Train came along and took that car clean out of my hand!"

Jimmy is five and Winton's brother, Charlie Nolan Dean, often comes over to the house and takes Jimmy riding on his "motorsickle." He sits Jimmy in front of him on the gas tank, between the handlebars, straps his big belt around him and off they go, thundering down the street. Jimmy shrieks with delight.

He begs Charlie Nolan to take him on a "real" trip, pesters him so much that Charlie seems to be thinking about it. Then Mildred breaks in to say she won't hear of it. It's too dangerous, and besides, Jimmy would dirty his clothes on those filthy old bikes. Sometimes Charlie Nolan brings one of his riding buddies along, an electrician named Marvin Carter, who doubles as a motorcycle mechanic. Ten years later, Marvin will sell Jimmy his first machine.

In 1936, Jimmy is six and the government transfers Dental Technician Winton Dean to a permanent staff position at the Sawtelle Veterans Administration Hospital in Los Angeles. The Deans are to be cut from their Indiana roots and set down on the shallow concrete sprawl of urban California.

Winton and Mildred and Jimmy say good-bye to the Winslows, good-bye to Grandpa and Grandma Dean. They ship their furniture west by Railway Express and set off in their new secondhand Nash.

A place to live isn't so hard to find in 1936. Rents aren't so ridiculous. The Deans move into a small, comfortable house in a middle-class Santa Monica neighborhood: stucco, Spanish tile, palm trees, one-car garages.

Jimmy is six. He sends the folks back in Fairmount a snapshot that shows him standing in front of a cabbage palm, squinting into the sun, still loyally wearing his Indiana overalls and holding tightly to his farmer's straw hat.

Other photos follow: Jimmy, now in a long-trousered jump suit, stands on the sidewalk beside the house, conspicuously not holding hands with a black-banged girl in a striped sweater. Jimmy, in short-sleeved knit shirt, big belt buckle, dark trousers, squats under a tree to irrigate the lawn with a toy water pump. The beginnings of self-consciousness show. He is smirking.

In September 1937, Jimmy becomes a first-grader at Brentwood Public School. He learns more in the yard than he does in the classroom. The other kids kid him about his Hoosier twang. They kid him about his funny middle name, which they wouldn't even know if his mother didn't insist on using it. "Hello, James Byron," the kids jeer. "Good-bye, James Byron. What's my name, James Byron?" Over and over again, Jimmy tells them his name is Deanie. That's what his father calls him. But they keep up the racket. They razz him, too, about his violin. Mildred has decided that he should have private musical instruction after school. Actually, Jimmy likes to practice, but he doesn't dare admit it to the kids.

At home, Jimmy's life is happier. Winton and Mildred don't want to spoil their son, but he is their only child and he gets all the love and attention they can give. They take him to the park for pony rides. They take him for drives up and down the Pacific Coast Highway. They see to it that he has plenty of books and toys.

Jimmy begins to show virtuosity on the violin. Mildred becomes convinced that she is raising a genius. She praises him when he does well, supports him during fits of failure. Winton encourages Jimmy, too, but most of the day he is away at the Veterans Hospital. Jimmy is not exactly the son he had imagined himself having. He wishes the kid would get involved in sports, even, perhaps, in a few fistfights.

Jimmy is doing well, running the gantlet of childhood torments and traumas, and then, one spring (May 1940), the pains Mama has been complaining of get so bad that she is taken away to the hospital. Winton writes to his mother in Fairmount, telling her that Mildred has terminal cancer. Emma Dean takes the letter to her doctor. He tells her that in all probability Mildred has only six or eight weeks to live. She leaves immediately for Los Angeles to take care of her daughter-in-law's child, husband, and household. On July 14, 1940, after terrible suffering, Mildred dies.

Her death leaves Jimmy embittered and abandoned. Later, he will say: "My mother died on me when I was nine years old. What does she expect me to do? Do it all alone?"

After the funeral service in Santa Monica, Emma Dean gives her son a message from his sister Ortense and her husband Marcus. "Now, Winton," Emma says, "I want you to think this over carefully. If you see fit to let Jimmy come back to Fairmount, Ortense and Marcus would like to take him. They'll raise him for you, if you want.". She goes on to argue that it would be nice for the Winslows to have a boy on the farm. Markie Jr., their own son, has not yet been born.

Winton Dean doesn't say anything for a while. He just stares through his rimless lenses. He doesn't have a single relative in California, no one there he can really count on. What would happen if he got sick, if Jimmy got sick? Worst of all he has to be away from the house from early in the morning till six or seven in the evening. The idea of remarrying is far from his thoughts. The pain of Mildred's death is too great.

Emma gives Winton plenty of time to think it over. At last, he begins to speak. "You can't find a finer man than Marcus Winslow, and as far as choosing between the way my sister would mother Jimmy and how some house-keeper might take care of him, there's just no question."

Winton decides to let Emma take Jimmy back to Indiana. She agrees that it's the right choice. As it turns out, Jimmy would have been uprooted eighteen months later anyway. In late 1942, Winton will be drafted into the Army Medical Corps.

So, after seven weeks in California (how accurate her doctor's diagnosis of Winton's letter had been), Emma Dean gets on the train with her nine-year-old grandson and the body of her daughter-in-law to make the long trip back to Indiana. Every time they stop at a big station, Jimmy gets off and runs forward to the baggage car to make sure his mother's casket is still aboard.

Back in Indiana, Grandpa Dean finds a plot for his daughter-in-law in the Grant Memorial Park Cemetery just south of Marion. Mildred will be buried there under a small, plain slab that reads: WIFE, MILDRED MARIE DEAN, September 15, 1910–July 14, 1940.

From the very first night Jimmy arrives at the farm, the Winslows do everything they can to help him get over his mother's death. "We wanted him," says Ortense. "He was so cute we just loved him." On the second night at the farm, Jimmy cries himself to sleep in their big bed. He seems to feel safe there. They give him their bedroom and move across the hall. Grandma Dean approves when she comes to visit: "The bed was maple and that seemed right for a boy."

As the months go by, Emma Dean grows more and more certain that she did the right thing in bringing her grandson back from California. "I don't mean to brag," she will say, "but Ortense and Marcus are a daughter and son-in-law any woman would be proud to own. They do their share in the community, and, besides their organizations, Ortense plays the piano for the Friends' Sunday School and Marcus is interested in Earlham College, a Quaker school near here. Both are wise and gentle and have a great gift for loving. Theirs is like a Quaker home should be. You never hear a harsh word. Best of all, they are happy as well as good—and that's what Jimmy needed most after the shock of losing his mother.

Jimmy's face is changing. In his bright feathered Alpine hat and dark zipper jacket, he tries to smile into the camera. His mouth makes it halfway. His eyes don't make it at all. Their innocence is breeched. They are asking questions to which they suspect there are no answers.

The early-to-bed, early-to-rise routine of the farm gives Jimmy little time, at least by day, to brood over the loss of his mother and the separation from his father. He and his cousin Joan are up by six o'clock for breakfast and chores. A little before eight, they must be out on the road to catch the big yellow school bus.

TWO

Fairmount, Indiana, is plain Main Street U.S.A., but some of its business buildings, such as the belly-windowed, golden-domed bank, are kept well enough painted and polished to make the visitor suspect that the whole town might just have been put up on a movie lot.

There are two barber shops, a pool hall with adjoining bar, a drugstore, a drivers' license bureau, a supermarket, several gas stations. Farther out Main there are big white family houses sitting back on broad lawns. When Jimmy came back to Fairmount in 1940, people could still afford to live in those houses. Now most of them have been converted to funeral homes, doctor complexes, real estate offices, florist shops, beauty parlors.

Fairmount School, where Jimmy joined the fourth grade, was known to townspeople as "The Academy." Red brick, tall windows, a black roof gathering to a stone-trimmed tower, it still sits atop a rise at the west end of town, an abandoned fortress.

After Brentwood Public School, The Academy must

have seemed oppressive and gloomy. California's sunlit pastel walls had been replaced by dark-stained wood paneling, yellowing plaster rising to dim globed lights full of dead flies, floors the janitor had oiled so often they were almost black. The only bright places in the whole classroom were the shiny suns and moons that generations of backs and bottoms had polished out of the mahogany stained seats. In the top right-hand corner of each desk there was a hole for an inkwell that had long since disappeared. Books were kept in a shadowy space underneath.

Mrs. India Nose taught the fourth grade mornings. Mr. Ivan Seward took the class afternoons. Jimmy's first day was difficult. He cried. He had trouble with subtraction. The boy sitting behind him, Jerry Garner, took pity on the terrified newcomer, squeezed into the seat beside him and helped with the problem. Jimmy never forgot. When Jerry, who left The Academy for another grade school, returned to Fairmount High as a freshman, Jimmy, by then an established member of the class, shepherded him through the first uncertain days.

Even as a boy of ten, Jimmy didn't hang around much after school. "He lived way out on the farm," Garner recalls. "That's one thing, but he just didn't have too many close friends. He didn't have any enemies either. After a while he settled down like the rest of us, just an average kid, except that sometimes he did what you might call dumb things, stunts, I mean, to attract attention. I'm sure that had something to do with his mother dying like that when he was so young."

After school, Jimmy would take the bus back out to the

farm and work on one of his 4-H projects. The first year he kept baby chicks. Aunt Ortense, who, along with all her other chores, was raising chickens, showed him how.

The second year, Uncle Marcus let Jimmy have a small garden plot. He cultivated, planted, and tended it all by himself. Marcus also gave him the runt of a sow's litter. Jimmy bottle-fed the little pig up to normal size and, in the process, it became a pet. Grandma Dean remembers seeing Jimmy and his dog tearing across the barnyard with the pig squealing behind, trying to catch up. Later, Jimmy raised cattle. One of his Guernsey bulls won the Grand Champion's Blue Ribbon at the Grant County Fair.

Supper at the farm was early, five-thirty, six o'clock. Uncle Marcus, whom the hired hands called "Rack," would come in from the fields. Sometimes the hired men would eat with the family. Sometimes Joan would invite one of her girl friends home from school to stay overnight. Supper was the biggest and best meal of the day. Ortense could really cook—roasts, steaks, chops, fish, vegetables, soups, salads, bread, cakes, and pies. Sometimes the long days in the kitchen made her arthritic fingers ache. Years later, when he came back from New York or Hollywood, Jimmy would talk of moving Ortense to a drier climate where her hands wouldn't hurt so much.

After supper, Jimmy did his homework. Then he would read for a while or listen to the radio, or do both at once. Ortense would come up, tuck him in, kiss him good night, turn out the light. Sometimes, although it was forbidden, he would take the radio down off the bedside table, turn it on low, and press it to his ear. At night he could hear stations as far away as Baltimore or New York. Often he fell asleep listening to music and woke up next morning to find his ears full of hog and steer prices from an Indianapolis station which had regained command of the local ether.

Marcus and Ortense Winslow gave Jimmy a lot of time and attention, occasionally even more than they gave to their own daughter, Joan, or to their own son, Markie Jr., who was born in 1943, three years after Jimmy came to the farm. "Jimmy was such an unusual child, he kind of demanded it," Ortense Winslow explains.

Grandma Dean noticed, too, that her grandson was unusual. "If Grandpa Dean sat with his legs crossed, Jimmy crossed his; if Grandpa stretched his legs out, Jimmy did, too. It was more than just mocking Grandpa's gestures. Even then, Jimmy seemed able to be another person."

When Cousin Joan was given dancing lessons, Aunt Ortense encouraged Jimmy to learn as well. When he got straight A's in art, she arranged drawing lessons for him with Indiana landscape painter Mary Carter. When he showed an interest in music, she tried to teach him to play the piano, but soon discovered that she couldn't coax him out of the barnyard and into the living room. Ortense didn't give up. She bought him a clarinet. He took to it immediately. Then he asked for a set of drums. When he got them he practiced by the hour without any urging at all. Later, in high school he drummed with the band and with a pick-up group that played for dances around Grant County.

And Uncle Marcus saw to it that Jimmy learned all

the things he knew. One of Jimmy's classmates told Grandma Dean: "I always envied Jimmy. My dad never took time to play with me, but Marcus was forever out there shooting baskets with Jimmy or passing a football or taking him hunting or showing him how to do stunts." Fairmount farmers rarely encouraged kids to come on their land except to work. Marcus went out of his way to make his farm a playground. In the winter he would run an electric line from the barn down to the frozen gravel pit pond and string lights in the trees so the kids could skate after dark. Jimmy and his friends could build a fire, drink cider, toast marshmallows, but cigarette smoking and beer drinking were strictly forbidden.

Marcus let the kids play in the barn, too. With Whitey Rust, a boy who lived down the road in the house next to the Back Creek Friends' Church, Jimmy built a labyrinth of tunnels in the hay. When it was finished, Jimmy and Whitey invited the boys out from school to play hide and seek. Since they knew the hay maze by heart they could stay hidden as long as they liked. Once they even let the other boys go home mad without finding them.

Sometimes, Jimmy and Whitey made go-carts by screwing casters onto big wooden boxes. Then, after setting up long steep plank ramps from the hay loft, they would race—Jimmy did his first daredevil driving in Uncle Marcus' barn.

In the spring, Jimmy and Whitey would get out their .22's and shoot turtles in the gravel pit pond. Whitey loved turtle meat. Jimmy did too, but he didn't like shooting frogs—they were good for the pond. Besides, no one ate them. (In that era, Fairmount was still innocent of TV gourmet recipes such as frogs legs Provençal.)

But Whitey knew that Jimmy's eyes weren't too good, especially for distance. Just to be ornery, he would point at a frog's head popping out of the pond and yell, "Git him, Jim!" Jimmy would fire, occasionally scoring a hit. When he saw that it was a frog he had killed, he would go wild with anger. Whitey would laugh and tell Jimmy he'd damn well better get himself a new pair of specs if he ever intended to become a world champion turtleman.

Often enough, Jimmy did get new glasses, not so much for a change of prescription but because he had lost or broken his old ones by pulling some stunt, like diving into a pond head first to see how deep it was. Ruth Mac-Donald, the town optometrist, almost always had frames or lenses on order for Jimmy, and when he began to play basketball, she made him special prescription goggles.

THREE

As Jimmy got near driving age, which in Indiana is sixteen, his attention shifted from animals to machines. Uncle Marcus taught him to run the big tractor, and soon he was harrowing and harvesting with the hired hands. Then Marcus bought him a whizzer, a bike with a motor, a very loud motor, according to Grandma Dean: "You could hear Jimmy coming three miles away."

But it was not long before Jimmy wanted something less noisy and more powerful than a whizzer. Marvin Carter, Uncle Charlie Nolan's old riding buddy, had opened a bike shop down the road in an abandoned one-room school house. Jimmy had seen just the motorcycle he wanted. Finally, Marcus gave in.

Jimmy began to spend his afternoons at Marvin Carter's, which, by virtue of a warm welcome and a big red Coke machine, became a clubhouse for all the bike men and boys in the countryside. Carter was a tall, powerful man who wore plain white shirts and canvas pants pegged for riding. He was bright and blunt. Jimmy liked him. "He was in and out a lot," Carter remembers. "I used to kid him about that little motorsickle. He'd go down the road, go by here and never even wave, and he'd go home, and pretty soon he'd be right back up here. And I'd say, well, why don't you turn that on once in a while? He had a single, and it was a two cycle and it made a lot of noise—he had a big funnel on the end of it. And that bike could run pretty close to fifty, say, fifty-five. It was a 125cc. And I'd say, Jimmy, why don't you ever open 'er up? And he'd say, well, you know, Carter, I never ride very hard. And I'd say, well, you got just one speed, Jimmy, one speed. One Speed Dean, that's what I called him. And he'd just laugh.

"Jimmy was a nice kid and nobody really understood him, due to the fact that, well, a lot of people thought he was a smartie. Just like I said, if Jim come up here, if he was livin' today, why he'd just walk in and he might not even smile, even say boo. He'd walk on back to the bench, pick up a tool, walk out, do something to his motorsickle, come back in, lay the tool back on the bench, not say boo, beanbags or nothin', and walk back on out. And maybe he'd get up to the door and he'd think of somethin', you know, like that, and he'd tell you a little joke or what somebody said, and he'd laugh and walk out. He was just that type of kid. You just had to know him.

"Back when Jimmy first started ridin', he was just a kid and all the guys liked him and he'd come in here and rattle off to them and they'd rattle off to him. And one time I had a public address system and he got to playin' with it. He'd never seen a motorsickle race in his life. He'd only heard the guys tell about it and we'd showed him pictures and he'd seen movies here, but he'd never actually seen a motorsickle race. Well, he set that speaker out there and he got in here in the corner and I'm telling you, he had everybody in a riot. He put on a race that you'd just never heard anything like it. Made noise with his mouth. Just raisin' hell. And the guys he had racin' were the guys that come out here, Bottsey, and Weaver, and Jones, and Fogelson, all of them. He'd line them up, you know, he knew they had six and eight in a race, and he'd woooh, wooooh, wooooooooh, like that, you know. It was terrific!"

Carter also admired Jimmy Dean for his Hoosier ingenuity. "Back in 1948, 1946, you got a lot of motorsickles that come in big crates, you know, and they had a lot of pretty good lumber in 'em, but you had to draw the nails out of 'em and stack 'em up. So Jimmy come up here once and said to me, 'Carter, I gotta have some money. I got a date and I've got to have two or three dollars. You got a job for me?' 'No,' I said, 'but I'll give you the money.' 'No,' he said, 'I want to work for it.' So I said, 'I don't know,' and I studied and studied and I said, 'Yeah, I've got a job for you.' So I took him out there and showed him that bunch of crates all piled up that had to have the nails drove out of 'em. So he said, 'Okay, I'll get on it right away.'

"And it was hotter that day than Billy be damned. So he went away and after a while he come back with another boy about his size and he said, 'Carter, you got a hammer I can borrow?' So I got him a hammer and a pair of pliers and a nail puller. So he went out there and pretty soon he come in and he wanted some rope or something and I told him where to get it and he went and got it. Well, after a little I went out there and right between the shop and the shed he'd strung up this piece of cardboard sort of like a roof, and the kid was settin' in the shade underneath it. And he had this kid takin' out the nails for him. And Jimmy come in later to buy that kid a Coke and took it out to him. And I said to him, 'Boy, I understand you, you're a pretty good man.' And he said, 'Well, I'm usin' my head. I don't have to give him that much and I get the remainder. I don't have to do anything, I'm just contracting!'"

For the years of World War II and the years immediately after, Jimmy's world, except for high school in Fairmount, was that one half mile of country road, Marvin Carter's Motorcycle Shop, Whitey Rust's house, the Back Creek Friends' Church, the Winslow farm.

Although Jimmy heard about the war on the radio, read about it in the paper and listened to talk about it around the dinner table, it all seemed very far away. There was no change in his life when his father entered the Medical Corps. The separation had already occurred. Even food rationing, which brought the war's impact home to most households in America, had little effect on the nearly self-sufficient Winslow farm where butchering, baking, and preserving went on as usual.

FOUR

In seventh grade, when Jimmy Dean's class moved from The Old Academy to the big high school on South Vine Street, he met someone who realized that he was not destined to spend the rest of his life in overalls.

Adeline Nall had come to Fairmount High in the fall of 1940 to teach French, Spanish, Speech, and Dramatics. That was just a few weeks after Grandma Dean had brought Jimmy home from California. Adeline was no stranger to the Indiana countryside. She had been born in Marion twenty-five years before the birth, in that same city, of her future pupil.

Adeline's father died when she was four. That helped her understand the anguish Jimmy experienced after his mother's death, the pain that lay just under the surface and which she, like Jimmy, concealed with a sort of brusque humor.

More than anything else in the world, Adeline wanted to be an actress, a great actress. After she graduated from Marion College, she married a brilliant but impractical man with a name—Darl Otto Nall—that would have done credit to an early silent film director, and moved to Chicago where her new husband became the director of a settlement house. Jane Addams often came to dinner there, and she encouraged the young couple. Darl felt he was making progress as a sociologist. Adeline put on plays, taught night school, got some good roles, and felt she was becoming a better actress. In 1933 a son was born.

Darl and Adeline struggled on together for seven more years. Then, one day, Adeline realized that they were just as poor as ever, that Darl's career was going nowhere, that her own career was going nowhere, and that their son, David, needed some clear air and open space to evolve in. So, in the summer of 1940, Adeline gave up Chicago and acting and marriage and brought her son home to Indiana and got herself a teaching job at Fairmount High.

Although she knew of Jimmy's existence from the very first year in Fairmount (like everyone else in town she heard about his mother's death in California and of his return to live with his aunt and uncle), she didn't actually get to know him until three years later when, as a seventh-grader, he came to her for help with a reading he was to give at one of Aunt Ortense's Women's Christian Temperance Union meetings.

As head of dramatics at Fairmount, Adeline's home room was number 21, on the second floor. Behind the teacher's desk a tall door opens into a long, narrow cloakroom. At the back of the cloakroom, there is a short flight of stairs that leads up onto the stage of the theatre-auditorium. The scars of hundreds of performances show on the walls. Insults, slogans, hearts, faces, names, initials are carved and painted everywhere. The ambiance is that of an old off-Broadway theatre, charged by the never completely dissipated energy of so much concentrated emotion. Out front, four hundred empty seats listen intently to the echo-amplified creaking of footfalls on stage.

Here, Adeline coached Jimmy for his first public performance. "The extremely dramatic selection, *Bars*, which had been chosen for the competition, seemed too advanced for a youngster," she says, "but anyway, we worked for several days." *Bars* purported to be the confession, from behind bars, of a drunkard who, under the influence of demon rum, had murdered another man in a bar. The moral: Spend your time at bars and you'll wind up behind them!

When Jimmy wondered what to do with his hands, Adeline suggested that he stand behind a chair, gripping it for dramatic effect (hand around the bars). The evening of the contest came. Jimmy surged out onto the platform, moved behind a chair, gripped it with both hands and spoke his piece in a firm, fierce voice. He knew he had done well. There was applause, but no prize, not even honorable mention.

The next morning, he confronted Adeline in her cloakroom. She had, he told her, without mincing words, wrecked his performance. Although the judges had not mentioned it specifically, he was sure that they had faulted him for using a prop. "That damned chair!" he shouted, so angry that he used a curse word in front of his teacher.

This burst of fury worried Adeline. It seemed out of proportion in one so young. Later that day, when she ran into Marcus Winslow in the Rexall Drugstore, she said hello, asked how Ortense was and then got to the point. Marcus smiled and told her not to worry about Jimmy. The boy just had to learn that he couldn't win 'em all.

Adeline and Jimmy got to know each other better when he took Beginning Spanish. He dozed through so many of the classes that she gave him a big fat "D." She noticed, however, that after school, when he worked for her in the theatre, he was always wide awake. He set lights, sewed costumes, painted flats, foraged for properties, helped conform scripts. Much more exciting—she was always on the lookout for good student actors— Jimmy was a natural on the stage. Even in the small roles she first trusted him with, he moved and spoke as though his lines and his movements were being born in his own brain.

During freshman year, each student in Citizenship and Vocations (called Careers by the kids) was assigned the task of writing an original playlet. Jimmy's piece—young man chooses right road even though wrong road looks brighter—was one of three chosen for presentation in the auditorium theatre. Adeline directed. Jimmy played one of the principal roles. Watching Jimmy perform, Adeline realized that he was going to be one of the stars of her future productions.

The sophomore play committee, which included

Jimmy, picked *Mooncalf Mugford*, a thirty-minute drama by Brainerd Duffield, Helen and Nolan Leary.

This catalogue description caught the committee's eye: "Old John Mugford is taunted and teased by neighborhood kids and called Mooncalf Mugford. His mind has strayed. He talks to friends long dead and spends days down by the ocean watching imaginary scaly green dragons lurking in the water. Etta, his wife, still loves and cares for him, despite his delusion that she is plotting against his life. Tabby, her neighbor, urges her to send the old man to a home, but Etta refuses. The strain, however, becomes too much for Etta. Bit by bit, the audience realizes that her mind, too, is beginning to wander. In the final scene, old John urges Etta to come into his world of dreams. Etta begins to see the world through John's eyes. When Tabby, the neighbor, brings Etta a basket of greens, Etta sees Tabby not as a friend but as a malicious, albeit funny, intruder. Tabby runs out in terror. The curtain falls on John and Etta happily on their way down to the shore to talk to the wind and the waves."

Adeline cast Jimmy as Mooncalf. The role, like the last one of his career—Jett Rink in the film *Giant*—called for him to play a man decades older than himself. Even at fifteen, he seemed to be able to make aging characters convincing. Perhaps it was his love for Grandpa Charlie Dean that gave him the skill. That same year, the Fairmount High Thespian Society, of which he was a newly elected member, chose him to portray another old man, Major Morris in *The Monkey's Paw*, a forty-minute thriller by W. W. Jacobs and Lewis N. Parker. "Major Morris mentions a monkey's paw. The superstition is that its possessor may have three wishes. Mr. White listens to the old soldier's warning that the paw has hitherto brought only disaster. The Whites are given the gruesome thing and Mr. White wishes for 200 pounds. A Mr. Sampson appears with the news that their son has been killed at work and that the firm as a mark of sympathy is sending 200 pounds. A second wish is that his son may be restored to life. There is a knock. The distraught mother tries to open the door. While she is doing this, the old man mutters a third wish: that his son may return to his grave. The door is opened. No one is there." Sheer melodrama, of course, but in some of the bits that Jimmy was to introduce into his later film work—throwing dollar bills over his father in *East of Eden*, for instance—we can see that his early stage experiences stood him in good stead.

Jimmy worked hard at being an actor. He worked even harder at being an athlete. In spite of his slightly less than average height—in his senior year he stood five feet seven and a half inches and was the shortest but one of the boys on the basketball team—he went out for every sport at Fairmount High.

Paul Weaver, who had himself graduated from Fairmount in 1940, came back in 1947 as Head of Athletics.

"Back then," he remembers, "it was popular to wear white T-shirts, jeans some, and corduroys, and that's the way I remember seeing Jim, with a crew-cut, you know, those short hair cuts just after World War II. He was a very, very clean-cut young fellow.

"Jimmy was a little different than most boys, but not

so much different from kids today. He was different in those days because, as I remember, he was often alone. For example, if the baseball team were to practice, often you'd see the kids coming together, in a car, or a pickup; but Jimmy would usually arrive alone.

"What I'm really saying, I guess, is that Jimmy was pretty much of an individualist. He didn't take instruction in baseball and in track as well as most young fellows. But in basketball he did. It is a team sport and he needed his teammates and he needed his coach. In basketball, he had just fair ability, quickness, speed, but perhaps not quite the ability he had in baseball and track. And Jimmy understood all that. So in basketball he was a good listener, he was coachable, and a good team man, and as a result the team and the coach helped him become a pretty good basketball player by 1948 standards. In those days his height was no problem. He played guard, and there were plenty of five-foot-eight-inch boys playing guard on high school teams.

"Jimmy was good at track and particularly at the pole vault. Ten feet, in 1947–48, in Fairmount, Indiana, in Grant County, was a pretty fair vault. Today, on the local level, for a high school boy it would be twelve feet. But in Jimmy's day the runway was cinders. You didn't get much traction. Too loose. And the pole was steel, not flexible at all.

"Jimmy was competitive, not that it was often visible. It wasn't. But I knew he had it within himself. During his senior year—I didn't hear him say this, but someone told me—he said that he would be graduating pretty soon and that he was going to be leaving little old Fairmount, you know, and he wasn't coming back until he was somebody.

"Jimmy wasn't the kind of a boy—well, in those days, a coach could put his arm around a boy, not, well maybe partly in affection, but partly just to get near to talk. And this was common, you know, in basketball. And in some other sports, maybe even football, I don't know. But I'm sure that I felt at the time that Jimmy felt uncomfortable. He'd just feel a little bit uncomfortable with you being that close. Maybe he wouldn't have been if we'd been alone. I don't know, but with others around he felt uncomfortable. And there might have been times when he didn't play as much as he thought he should have, of course, and when he was upset with me, but it didn't show, it didn't come out.

"I don't recall ever seeing him, like on dates, with girls. But around school, well, it was a small school and you couldn't hardly be in the school building without being around girls. There weren't any sororities or fraternities or anything. Kids didn't pin each other. They went on dates, some, sure. If it was their first date, why they might drive into the show, you know, to the county seat, that would be Marion. Most kids had their license by the time they were sixteen. But I always recall Jimmy riding his motorcycle and I don't ever remember seeing a girl on it.

"The game I can recall the best was when he was a senior, the last game he ever played as a high school boy. We played Marion. In those days, small county schools just didn't often beat the county seat. In the final game of what we call the Sectional Tournament a pretty good

Marion team beat Fairmount 40 to 34. Jimmy got 15 out of our 34 points. That was probably the one best game he ever played. He gave it everything he had."

The class yearbook, *Black & Gold,* liked his performance: "Jim Dean, brilliant senior guard, was one of the main cogs in the Quaker line-up this season."

Jimmy struggled desperately to excel at sports and he got much of the recognition he wanted; but all his determination and practice could only polish a slightly above average native gift. On stage, it was different. Without nearly as much will and effort, he displayed exceptional talent. Schoolmates who watched him perform, like Phyllis Cox and Jim Grindle, schoolmates who acted with him, like Barbara Leach and Bob Pulley, knew that Jimmy was really good. But no one, except Adeline Nall, his teacher and director, had the artistic insight and the theatrical experience to see that his work would stand out even among professionals. She speaks of him more as a colleague and a friend than as a student and advisee. "It was in the fall of his junior year that his work began to mature. The class play, *Our Hearts Were Young and Gay,* required considerable staging. Jimmy acted as assistant stage man and also played the part of Otis Skinner. He insisted on a practical porthole—not just a painted one— on the set. This he made."

In Jimmy's senior year, at the Halloween Carnival, David Nall, Adeline's son, Joan Jones, a member of the Thespian Society, and Jimmy, now president of the Thespians, presented "Coon with the Wind," a vaudeville skit set in the Civil War atmosphere of Margaret Mitchell's great novel. David and Joan were innocent, unsuspecting lovers. Jimmy played the rejected, revengeful villain, complete with derby, cape, mustache, and leer. The cider-sipping audience cheered and clapped, hooted and stomped.

When the curtain came down on the evening's last play —other Thespians performed *At the Stroke of Twelve* and *Nellie at the Pump*—a Frankenstein monster appeared in the audience. Boys shouted and socked each other. Girls giggled and shrieked. The monster thumped out of the auditorium into the jack-o'-lantern-lit, witch-and-hobgoblin-decorated corridors, stumbled as though it could hardly keep its balance, blundered into doors and walls. The get-up was so good that no one could guess who was inside. Finally, because Jimmy didn't show up to celebrate with the other actors, his classmates guessed that he was the monster. But the creature would not speak, could not speak, apparently, and at last it disappeared into the night.

Jimmy had made the outsize horror head from a shoe box, working it over with scissors, paste, and paint until it came to life. The pleasure he felt in creating the monster mask and the power he experienced in being the monster left deep marks in his memory. In his early New York acting days he often told friends about his high school "Frankenstein act." Sometimes, he would get out the mask itself, which he had kept as a souvenir of his success.

And he loved playing pranks as much as he loved playing parts. In fifth period, the first after lunch, Jimmy and one of his friends, another Jim (James Grindle, now an Indiana State Police officer), had Advanced Speech with Adeline Nall. Students would gather outside her room waiting for her to come up from the cafeteria and unlock the door. But the two Jims made an important discovery. By climbing up the back fire escape they could slip into the auditorium through an open window, cross the stage, and enter the classroom through the connecting cloakroom. Once inside, they would turn on the lights, open the door and let the other kids in.

When Adeline came up from lunch she would find the class already seated and ready to begin work. She would puzzle a moment, look at the class, at the door, and then back at the class. Silence, a few smiles, nothing unusual. Oh well, she must have left it open, too much on her mind. Tomorrow she would make absolutely sure she locked up before lunch.

Since Jimmy lived out on the farm, he would often stay over at Jim Grindle's house on the night of a big basketball game. The two boys would go straight home after school and take a one-hour nap. Then they would ask Mrs. Grindle to make them poached eggs on toast. Poached eggs, they believed, would give them extra power on the basketball floor.

Often, after the game, a third Jim, the Reverend James DeWeerd, an evangelist preacher who lived in Fairmount, would drive the boys back to his house to celebrate their victory or recover from their defeat. (The team won ten out of twenty-one games Jimmy's senior year.)

James DeWeerd was in his thirties, a stocky, handsome man with penetrating blue eyes and heavy lips. He had himself graduated from Fairmount High and was remembered by his classmates for his passionate and, sometimes, at least by Quaker or Wesleyan standards, shocking language. Jim DeWeerd liked to tell jokes. Jim DeWeerd often "said things," things other people only thought.

Later, as an adult, he was forced to convert such expressions of his sensual energy into the hyperbole of maxim and homily.

For Jimmy, who had not been exposed to many highly educated people (with the exception of Adeline Nall), James DeWeerd's peculiar combination of cultivation and cant was fascinating. And Jim DeWeerd was respected in Fairmount. That meant it was okay for a man to be in love with language, for a man to write poetry, for a man to put on a performance—Jim DeWeerd was, everybody said, one hell of a preacher! He could make people laugh, cry, tremble in fear. And in a town where many believed that cards, moving pictures and dancing were inventions of the devil, Jim DeWeerd was not afraid of being "fancy." Dinner at Jim's house meant silver, linen, candlelight, crystal, and classical music in the background. Afterward, the pastor would show the boys films he had taken of bullfights in Mexico. He was fond of lecturing his young admirers: "The more you know how to do," he would say, "the more things you experience, the better off you will be."

Sometimes, he would take the boys over to Anderson for a swim at the "Y." Sometimes, he would take them along on a preaching date. Once, sitting in a car in front of the church where he was to speak, he spotted a woman in slacks. "Boys, I'm gonna tell you one thing. If that lady walks into that church tonight, I'm gonna preach them slacks right off her."

One day, he took Jimmy and several of his classmates into Indianapolis to the Speedway. They met a driver named Cannonball Baker. They watched a practice run. On the way home in the car they talked about racing and death. In recalling the excursion DeWeerd said, "I taught Jimmy to believe in personal immortality. He had no fear of death because he believed as I do that death is merely control of mind over matter."

Sometimes, Jimmy would be DeWeerd's only dinner guest. Then Jimmy would tell the preacher his fears, his terrible dreams. Was he not bad? Was he not evil? Why else had his mother left him? Why else had his father sent him away? DeWeerd would counter his terror with soothing talk of salvation. He would urge Jimmy to seek the Saviour with all his might.

When they didn't go to DeWeerd's house after the game, the boys would go out on dates. Bob Pulley (now an Indiana Bell maintenance man) and Jimmy occasionally double-dated the Class of 1949 twins, Edith May and Ethel Faye Thomas. "Most of the time," Pulley remembers, "you'd go out to the drive-in, get something to eat. That'd be about it. Or you'd go out and park if you had one that would, and if you didn't, why, you'd go home."

And there were barn parties at which the kids danced, bobbed for apples, fooled around in the straw. The boys would show off with long Tarzan glides on a rope swung from the hayboom, or climb way up onto the highest beam and try to pour cider into the mouths of girls standing below.

And there were hay rides over still night roads, through snowy fields. Somebody had to drive the tractor, of course, but the lucky ones back in the wagon could tell jokes, smoke, neck or just stare at the moon and enjoy being out from under adult eyes for a few hours.

Like Grandpa Charlie Dean, Jimmy always kept busy. But for all his preoccupation with athletics, acting, and amusing himself, he still had energy left over for debating. His partner in the Debate Club was a pretty, dark-haired girl named Barbara Leach. "Barb," said the yearbook, "has eyes that always shine, and in her studies she does just fine!"

Jimmy and Barbara defended the negative view of the proposition: "Resolved that the United Nations be Revised into Federal World Government." They got so good at it that they were asked to debate Marion High School on a local radio station. On the Saturday before the big broadcast they went into Marion to gather more ammunition at the library. Afterward, Jimmy suggested that they walk up to the courthouse square "just to mess around a little bit."

But once they got to the square, Jimmy steered Barbara straight toward Resnick's, a jewelry store which had a long glass display case on the sidewalk just outside the entrance. Barbara wondered what Jimmy was up to.

He guided her to one end of the case and told her to

bend down and look along the glass. Then he went to the other end, raised one arm, and one leg, and to Barbara it looked as though he was raising both arms and both legs at the same time. She giggled with surprise. Jimmy laughed. When she asked him if he'd been there before to practice "that silly stunt," he just smiled. On the way home they stopped at a doughnut shop and bought a dozen warm doughnuts and ate all of them.

At the end of senior year Jimmy and Barbara went to a county debaters' banquet at Swayzee, or Sweetzer (Barbara doesn't remember which). She wore a dress made of material that looked something like burlap, and Jimmy teased her all evening about her "potato sack."

Jimmy's last play at Fairmount High was *You Can't Take It with You.* Adeline cast him as Boris Kolenkhov, the "mad Russian." She wanted him to play Grandpa Vanderhof, one of the leads, but since none of her other actors could breathe any life into the Kolenkhov role, she was forced to sacrifice her star in a minor part. "Nevertheless," Adeline remembers, "Jimmy played with all the verve of a veteran."

On opening night, in behalf of the class, Jimmy gave Adeline an orchid corsage. He helped her pin it on and then kissed her. Everybody clapped. Adeline cried. No previous class had made such a gesture. Even this class did not know it was Adeline's very first orchid. When the play went well, the evening seemed almost too good to be true.

Next day, Adeline put the orchid, a fragile reminder of the previous night's triumph, in a glass of water on her desk. Just before noon, Jimmy came in and asked to borrow it. Adeline wondered why. He would not say. After extracting a solemn promise that he would return the flower unharmed, she let him take it.

An hour later, he returned with the orchid in one hand and a rolled-up sheet of paper in the other. He spread the paper out in front of her. She could hardly believe her eyes. There, twice life-size, in subtle pastels, was her orchid. Beneath it were the words: "Her Pride." He knew the real flower would fade, Jimmy explained, so he had made her one she could keep forever. She felt tears in her eyes again.

The day after the play's second and last performance, Jimmy, Aunt Ortense, and Adeline drove to Peru, Indiana (Cole Porter's home town), where, at the high school, Jimmy competed in a state-wide speaking meet sponsored by the National Forensic League.

The second day of competition, his impassioned reading brought him the all-Indiana prize. He burst through the curtain with a bloodcurdling scream. Acting out the symptoms of hallucination, he brought his piece, Dickens' *The Madman,* to a climax by collapsing on stage. The judges were immensely impressed by his performance, even a bit frightened. One commented later on the odd glitter in the contestant's eyes.

Fairmount was impressed, too. The Fairmount *News* for Thursday, April 14, 1949, said in a bannerhead: "F.H.S. STUDENTS WIN STATE MEETS." Subhead: "James Dean First Place Winner in Dramatic Speaking." The other Fairmount winner was Adeline's son, David. She was doing well both as parent and drama coach.

Jimmy's win made him eligible to enter the national speaking tournament of the N.F.L. which was scheduled for April 29 and 30 in Longmont, Colorado. Everybody was proud that Fairmount High, in the person of Jim Dean, was going to represent the state of Indiana in an all America contest. A travel fund was quickly collected. The banker, the doctor, the druggist, the florist, and a number of businessmen and just plain people gave a total of $105 to send Jim and Adeline to Longmont.

On Thursday, April 28, 1949, the day before the contest, the Fairmount *News* ran a three-column front-page head: "Good Luck at Longmont, Jim!" And *News* readers got all the exciting details. "Jim and Mrs. Brookshire (Adeline had married again) began their journey Wednesday at 11:03 A.M. (CST) and arrived in Chicago at 2:30 P.M. Taking the Burlington Zephyr at 5:30 P.M. from Chicago, Jim and Mrs. Brookshire arrived in Denver, Col., at 8:30 A.M. Thursday. From Denver, the journey turned north and terminated in the city of Longmont at 10:00 A.M."

At the beginning of their three-hour layover in Chicago, Adeline suggested a walk around the city. She wanted to have a look at the neighborhood in which she had lived and worked years before. Jimmy didn't want to leave the station. He was afraid the train would pull out without them. Adeline finally convinced him that a famous train like the Zephyr wouldn't leave a second before or after the time printed on the official schedule, 5:30 P.M.

Not far from the station they found themselves on Halsted Street, Chicago's skid row. Suddenly Jimmy was tugging at Adeline's coat sleeve. He had never seen a bum before. The clots of ragged, red-faced, staggering men terrified him. Adeline could not get him to go on. She led him back to the station. She thought of setting off again by herself, but Jimmy was too upset to be left alone. He kept talking about those poor men. That night, as the Zephyr horned its way through the darkness, Jimmy twisted and turned in his seat. Every time he closed his eyes, he saw bleary faces, bloodshot eyes. He got up and paced the aisle until morning.

The tournament photographer happened to catch Adeline and Jimmy as they were signing in. Adeline, in a smart suit, bangs and girlish knit hat, could still, after all those hours of sitting up on the train, manage a smile for the registrars. But Jimmy's face was drawn, his eyes hollow. He stared glumly at the forms he would have to fill out.

The first days' rounds went well. But Adeline was worried. By her watch, Jimmy's piece was running at least two minutes over the ten-minute limit. Scanning the list of judges, she discovered that one of them was a former colleague.

During a break, she went up to this judge and asked her if the time limit would weigh heavily in the scoring. Guessing what was really on Adeline's mind, the judge said that she really liked Jimmy's work but that his first reading had, indeed, been too long. If all other factors were equal, overtime could make the difference between winning and losing. It could even eliminate a contestant from the finals.

Adeline went back into the auditorium and dragged Jimmy out by the ear. She told him what she had just learned. She showed him the cuts she had prepared for such an emergency, deletions which, she argued, with her own considerable debater's skill, would not only *not* damage the sense of the reading but actually increase its impact. "Short and sweet, Jim, that's the way to win." But Jimmy wouldn't listen. He was already an actor. He didn't want his part cut, not by a phrase, not by a single word.

That evening, after a bus tour of nearby Rockies, tournament guests were fed beef and beans at a big Chuck Wagon outing. Jimmy had never seen so many people. He hovered around Adeline, at times actually clinging to her arm. After dinner Adeline suggested that Jim "go off on his own a little and meet some of the other young people." He promptly disappeared into the crowd. She didn't see him again until he appeared in the finals next morning. Had he cut his speech? She kept one eye on her watch. No. Again, he ran two minutes over, perhaps even a few seconds longer than the day before. But his performance was better, so good that the audience broke into applause. She waited for the winners to be announced.

The judges read off the names. Jimmy's was not among them. He came rushing up to her with tears in his eyes. Choked by her own emotion, she couldn't speak. She led

Jimmy up to the friendly judge, introduced him. "Young man," said the judge, smiling, "you gave an excellent reading, but it was twelve minutes long. That's two minutes over the limit. I'm sorry." Jimmy was shattered. He couldn't even muster enough voice to thank the judge for her courtesy in explaining the decision.

On the train next day, Sunday, Jimmy stared out the window and refused to talk. Even though she was heartsick herself, Adeline decided to carry out her previously made plan to stop off at Denver for some sightseeing. Who could tell when she would have a chance to get down that way again?

She took Jimmy to Red Rocks Park to see the mammoth natural amphitheatre that Mary Garden once proclaimed the acoustical equal of any opera house in Europe or America. Jimmy, in spite of his low spirits, could not resist getting up on the great stage and shouting a few lines from his *Madman* speech. Later, at Buffalo Bill's grave on Lookout Mountain, he stooped down and, after asking —in a whisper—the dead hero's permission, pocketed several souvenir pebbles. He could not have suspected, in the middle of his eighteenth year, that only six years later, dozens of film pilgrims would be chiseling chips from his own tombstone.

Knowing, although he could not admit it to Adeline, that his defeat at Longmont had been his own fault, he was particularly afraid of what people would say when he got home. But no one kidded him. Uncle Marcus said for the thousandth time: "You can't win 'em all." His classmates could see that he was suffering quite enough without their help.

Besides, the class was busy getting ready for its six-day trip to Washington. All year the seniors had been raising money. They held "Penny Suppers" in the cafeteria (low-admission dinners for which mothers provided most of the food free), they sold hot dogs at farm auctions, they peddled magazine subscriptions door to door. There had even been a small profit on the class play. By April they had banked $1,760.00.

Joyce John, who, next to Jimmy, was Adeline's favorite pupil, kept an awestruck diary of the trip. The class visited the Lincoln Memorial, the Washington Cathedral, the Smithsonian, and took a: "40 mile tour down Potomac on a huge steam boat. Name of boat is Mount Vernon. Love the 'salt spray' blowing in our faces. Believe this is the high point of trip. Lot of lights twinkling on the shore. Can see the Capitol Dome and Washington Monument 'way off in distance."

She didn't tell her diary that "our faces" meant hers and Jimmy's. They had slipped away from the dance and gone up on deck for a long romantic talk about the future. She didn't tell her diary, either, that the very next night Jimmy and some of his buddies bargained a bottle from a bellboy and got roaring drunk in their hotel room. Perhaps she never found out about the incident, or perhaps she simply wanted to make certain that no news of it got back to the sober Quaker community of Fairmount.

When the forty-nine members of the class of '49 got home, they had just four days of high school left in their lives. Soon they would have only their memories and their yearbook: "May 16 we were graduated and our school life was ended but we will always remember our times at Fairmount High School." Under "Footsteps on the Sands of Time," Jimmy willed: "My short temper to David Fox," a boy he had once punched for making fun of him in speech class. In a facetious forecast of the future, one of Jimmy's drawings had brought him a curious kind of fame: "Jim Dean has his masterpiece of Barbara Leach hanging in Carnegie Hall." Did they mean the Metropolitan?

Several times before graduation, Jimmy had gone West to see his father and stepmother. Winton Dean had gotten out of the Army in 1945 and returned to his job as supervisor of the dental lab at the Sawtelle Veterans Administration Hospital in Los Angeles. In that same year he had remarried. Ethel Case became the second Mrs. Dean.

Occasionally, too, Winton had come to Indiana to see his relatives and his son. But strangely enough, not one of Jimmy's friends can remember seeing Jimmy and his father together. Apparently, Winton never came to see Jimmy act, or debate, or play basketball.

He was, nevertheless, concerned about Jimmy's future. In the spring of Jimmy's senior year, he began to write letters telling his son that after graduation he expected him to come to California to live. He also forwarded college entrance applications. He wanted Jimmy to enter Santa Monica City College as a pre-law student. Such a career choice seemed indicated by the things he had heard about Jimmy's skills in public speaking and debate.

Jimmy filled out the papers, sent them back to Santa Monica and forgot all about them. His schedule of classes, games, plays, debates, readings, trips, kept him far too busy to think of anything but getting through the very next day. Besides, with his barely average grades, he could hardly expect any college to admit him.

Then, just a few days after getting his diploma, when he was looking forward to taking it easy for a while, a letter came from Winton telling him that he had been admitted to Santa Monica City College. There was only one condition. He would have to attend summer school so he could start off in the fall on an equal academic footing with better-prepared students from the big Los Angeles schools. Students were to report for the summer session in the first week of July.

Jimmy could hardly believe it. In a few days he would have to say good-bye to Aunt Ortense and Uncle Marcus, to Markie Jr., to his motorcycle, to the cows, sows, chickens, dogs, cats, trees, fields, ponds, streams, sheds, and barns he had lived with for nine years. It sounded long when you said it. But it went by fast when you lived it.

The Winslows took him to Marion in their new Ford, hugged him, put him on the train, cried, and waved. From behind the thick glass Jimmy waved back. As the train raced across fields bright with early summer sun, he knew his Indiana boyhood was over.

He thought about his new life in California. In college, he would really have to hit the books. Athletics and acting and clowning around weren't going to get him through pre-law. He remembered, too, that he would have to get in touch with the Santa Monica draft board. He had registered in Fairmount on his last birthday, February 8, 1949, his eighteenth. Fairmount would forward his papers.

Some of the people who knew Jimmy thought his terribly nearsighted eyes got him a 4-F classification. Others think he was saved by the fact that there were enough other boys in perfect physical condition to fill local quotas. Others think that he registered as a conscientious objector. He had, after all, been raised as a Quaker. Still others, including an ex-official of the Fairmount Selective Service Unit, and one of Jimmy's closest Hollywood friends, say he told the draft board: "You can't draft me. I'm homosexual."

FIVE

The Sawtelle Veterans Administration Hospital spreads over hundreds of West Los Angeles acres between Westwood and Brentwood. On its way to Santa Monica and Pacific Ocean, Wilshire Boulevard cuts through the south end of the gigantic reservation. North and south, the San Diego Freeway slices through it, separating the living, in dozens of four-story brick wards, from the dead, bedded down under row after row of look-alike white crosses. The city swirls around the Sawtelle Hospital, barely aware of its existence.

The buildings are identified by number. The streets have names: Eisenhower, Pershing, Grant, Washington. There is a post office, a news stand, a cafeteria, and a place to sit on the worn grass under the trees and listen to music coming out of staticky loudspeakers. The old soldiers who can still walk, do. They look up at passing cars without curiosity. They know they aren't going anywhere. Those who can't walk lie in their rooms or their wards, waiting for an occasional visitor, for an occasional package from the outside world. The proprietor of a Mexican basket shop near the hospital remembers delivering papers inside the hospital when he was a boy. He never knew what he was going to see when he opened a door. Some men had no arms; others had no legs; some were just bundles of bandages with eyes peering out.

The dental laboratory which Winton Dean supervised lay south of Wilshire Boulevard in the Wadsworth, a group of older wooden buildings with slanting roofs and long screened porches. Sitting among tall palms, they looked like holdovers from the Cuban and Philippine campaigns of the Teddy Roosevelt era. Two years ago, Wadsworth was wiped out by a big fire; a few palms and some smaller outbuildings remain.

Three blocks west of the hospital compound, on Saltair Avenue, Winton and Ethel had rented a house, number 1527½. There was an extra room. In the spring of 1949, they got it ready for Jimmy, and when he arrived from Indiana, they did their best to make him feel at home. But the contrast between the "cute" little cottage in West Los Angeles and the great Winslow farmhouse dominating hundreds of windy Indiana acres was striking. So was the contrast between the strong, simple Winslows and the cautious, complicated Deans. The years of separation had turned Jimmy and his father into strangers, and he hardly knew his stepmother at all.

The person Jimmy would come to feel closest to in this period was Gene Owen, chairwoman of the Drama Department at Santa Monica City College. In 1949, the col-

lege had not yet moved to its new campus on Pico and
Twentieth and still shared grounds with Santa Monica
High School, which, under the name Dawson High,
Jimmy and Nicholas Ray would use five years later as
one of the principal locations in *Rebel Without a Cause.*

Unfortunately, sharing the same physical plant meant
that neither college nor high school had permanent use
of the theatre. Classroom acting experiments, classroom
readings were the rule. But even in the classroom, Mrs.
Owen spotted Jimmy's talent. She particularly liked him
as Hamlet: "He had an extraordinary perception of the
role," she says, "electrifying and different. I was staggered by his work with the soliloquies."

Gene Owen taught Jimmy History of Theatre, Beginning Acting, Voice and Diction, and Radio. In the drama
courses, Jimmy got A's and B's. In his pre-law subjects,
he got C's and D's.

Although the Drama Department couldn't provide
much opportunity to work on stage, it did maintain a radio station. Jimmy tried some announcing, read parts in
plays, and hung around listening to other people's programs. One night Mrs. Owen dropped in at the station
while a student comedy team, Fred and Mackie, was
doing a spoof of the Canadian Royal Mounties. Through
the control-room window she saw Jimmy, an attentive
audience of one, sitting in the studio, laughing at every
gag.

An important part of Jimmy's rapidly evolving talent
was his responsiveness to other people's talents. He was
always watching, listening, appraising. Much of his origi-

nality, his freshness, came from his big collection of stored-away images. Sometimes, he liked to talk as well as look and listen. Mrs. Owen would return to her office in an old converted library building to find Jimmy sitting on top of her radiator like a pet cat. Then she knew he wanted conversation, and if she had the time, they would talk, for hours and hours. It soon became painfully evident that he had even less formal education than she had imagined, but she could not help being impressed by his amazingly bright mind, and his exceptional talent for theatre. She began to feel great affection for this shy, confused, gifted boy.

Toward the end of his freshman year at Santa Monica, Jimmy decided to transfer to UCLA. As gently but firmly as she knew how, Mrs. Owen counseled him against the change. But she could not articulate most of her argument for fear of hurting Jimmy's feelings. She felt that he would be overwhelmed academically, that he was not ready for the relentless competition of UCLA's huge Theatre Arts Department, that he needed a more intimate setting in which he could have one-to-one relationships with his teachers. But he decided that he had to make the move. He wanted to work on a stage. UCLA had Royce Hall, a completely equipped theatre. UCLA staged real productions, as good and sometimes better than anything else in Los Angeles.

To put together money for the coming year, Jimmy took a summer job as an athletic instructor at a military academy. In the fall, he entered UCLA. Still trying to fulfill his father's wishes, he signed up for a pre-law major, a Theatre Arts minor, and he joined a fraternity, Sigma Nu. But his house dues, his tuition, books, and what few clothes he bought always added up to more than he could put in the bank. The University Employment Bureau gave him occasional work as a projectionist for professors who used film in their courses.

Life at the fraternity house wasn't easy, either. One member of Sigma Nu remembers: "I was a junior in 1950. I first met Jimmy Dean during rushing in the fall semester. My first impression was that he was quite sincere. Well, he pledged and then it became quite apparent after a couple of weeks that the controls that are exerted over a pledge were just a little—he just couldn't accept them —things like missing the Monday night meetings. But Jimmy finally did get initiated into the house, even though there was some talk as to whether he should have to go through another semester of pledging and then go through pre-initiation week, but they finally decided to let him go through. And at this time, he had his final bit of trouble, I guess you'd say, and it ended up with a fist fight."

At one of the fraternity beer brawls, several of Sigma Nu's older members began telling Jimmy about the humiliating and infantile tasks he would be expected to perform during pre-initiation week. Jimmy told them point-blank what they could do with their initiation. They got angry and began heckling him about being in the Theatre Arts Department, which, they said, was exclusively for sissies, if not pansies. Jimmy slugged one of his tormentors and walked out of the house. He never came back.

A few days later, on a bus coming home from Holly-wood, where he had been making the rounds for TV and film parts, he ran into Bill Bast, a Theatre Arts major in his junior year. He suggested that they look for an apartment together. Jimmy had met Bill during a Royce Hall pro-duction of *Macbeth* in which Jimmy and Bill's girl friend, Joanne, had both been cast. The Theatre Arts Depart-ment magazine, *Spotlight*, had been unenthusiastic about the production in general and about Jimmy's perform-ance in particular: "Malcolm (James Dean) failed to show any growth and would have made a hollow king." Joanne was not even accorded the courtesy of a mention.

Shortly after that first meeting, Jimmy, who was still a pledge in good standing at Sigma Nu, had tried to get Bill into the fraternity. But Bill had muffed his first cru-cial get-together with "the boys" and was forced to go on living in a dormitory.

Bill gave Jimmy's apartment-sharing proposition some concentrated consideration. Perhaps rooming with Jimmy would be a good idea. For one thing, the dormitory was getting unbearable. For another, Jimmy had qualities—self-reliance, drive, independence—which he wouldn't mind acquiring and probably could acquire if he got a chance to study them at close range. Thirdly, Jimmy had just been signed by a Hollywood agent and probably wouldn't mind giving him an introduction. Hadn't Jimmy worked hard to get him into Sigma Nu? Why not try it? Bill and Jimmy shook hands on the deal.

Jimmy was so happy that Bill hadn't rejected his idea that he delivered himself of one of his more manic ego manifestoes: "Have you ever had the feeling that it's not in your hands?" he asked. Bill nodded obligingly. "I mean," Jimmy went on, "do you ever just know you've got something to do and you have no control over it? All I know is, I've got to do something. I don't know exactly what it is yet. But when the time comes, I'll know. I've got to keep trying until I hit the right thing. See what I mean?" Again, Bill nodded. "It's like I want to be an actor, but that isn't it. That's not all. Just being an actor or a director, even a good one, isn't enough. There's got to be more than just that. I figure there's nothing you can't do if you put everything into it."

Bill kept nodding. He was beginning to feel the hypnotic effects of Jimmy's stream of words. "If you start accepting the world, letting things happen to you, around you, things will happen like you never dreamed they'd happen. That's why I'm going to stick to this thing. I don't want to be just a good actor. I don't even want to be just the best. I want to grow and grow, grow so tall nobody can reach me."

Jimmy talked on and on, getting higher and higher, pumping himself up on his own words. "To me, the only success, the only greatness for man, is immortality. To have your work remembered in history, to leave something in this world that will last for centuries. That's greatness. I want to grow away from all this crap, the petty world we exist in. There's a level somewhere where everything is solid and important. I'm going to try to reach up there and find a place I know is pretty close to perfect."

At nineteen, it's not hard to get drunk on dreams. It's hard to carry them out when you sober up again. But Jimmy was different. He put lots of everyday, down-to-earth effort into his career.

Agent Isabelle Draesmer had seen Jimmy's Malcolm and liked his performance more than the *Spotlight* reviewer. She had gone backstage, complimented him on his work, left her card. He called her the next day and drove up to Hollywood for an interview. She signed him and began sending him up for parts. And he looked for roles on his own. He scanned *Daily Variety, Hollywood Reporter,* made phone calls, hung out at Schwab's drugstore, tried to get in to see producers, badgered casting directors.

The day after their chance meeting on the bus, Jimmy and Bill cut classes to look for an apartment. They wanted something in Santa Monica near the beach, but everything they saw was either too small or too expensive. Toward the end of the day, when they had almost given up, a pleasant-faced, middle-aged woman showed them a bachelor flat which was so dark and cramped that they rejected it the minute they stepped through the door.

She took pity on the two sad-eyed young men, led them up an outside stair to the roof of the building and showed them a small penthouse she had not intended to rent. Its three rooms were done in a collage of Spanish, Mexican, and Indian styles with a fillip of Italian influence for good measure. The rent wasn't outrageous, but there was a condition. The woman explained that she was the holder of a Master of Fine Arts degree from the University of West Virginia and that the penthouse was her pet decorating project. If the boys were going to live there they would have to leave things exactly as they were and, of course, keep the place clean and neat. Jimmy put on a tremendous show of enthusiasm. He tried a chair, bounced on a bed, turned on the shower, opened the refrigerator, put his head in the oven, peered out a window and ended this Goldilocks routine by flinging himself down in the middle of the living-room rug and smiling up at his landlady-to-be with boyish delight. The penthouse was theirs. But paying the first month's rent in advance left them almost broke.

In New York, at what was then called Idlewild Airport, Ben Alcock, an account man on Pepsi-Cola at the Milton Biow agency, boarded a four-motor Constellation for Los Angeles. He was going to the Coast to okay some kids the Jerry Fairbanks organization had gotten together for a new series of TV commercials. Arriving in L.A., Ben and his wife, Susan, who had come along to escape the East Coast cold for a few days, checked in at the Beverly Hills Hotel and did some star gazing in the Polo Lounge. Next morning, they got up early, called for their rented car and drove up to Griffith Park where, at the merry-go-round, one of the commercials was scheduled to start shooting later in the day.

Fairbanks lined up dozens of Clairol-blond California kids for Alcock to look at. For "the lead," he picked a boy whose smile shone out from all the rest—sunny, sweet and at the same time, sad and mysteriously engaging. Mrs. Alcock seconded her husband's choice. The part was simple: passing big, frosty twelve-full-ounces-that's-a-lot bottles to shrieking, squealing kids as they spun into frame on their crazy-colored carousel mounts. Somehow that young man's smile seemed to hold up take after take. It was a great day's shooting. Years later, thumbing through a *Look* photo spread in his dentist's waiting room, Ben Alcock realized that the kid he had put into the Pepsi spot was Jimmy Dean. It was Jimmy's first appearance on film.

The Santa Monica penthouse provided Jimmy and Bill with their first experience of grown-up privacy. They could sit up and talk until dawn. They could read forbidden books without fear of censure or confiscation. Jimmy thought it was a gas to read the steamier passages of Henry Miller's *Sexus* to girl friends who came over to party with the young bachelors in their rooftop retreat.

The new freedom brought more of Jimmy's subconscious to the surface. In Fairmount, he had drawn an orchid for Adeline Nall, sculptured a small, brooding figure called "Self" for James DeWeerd. In Santa Monica, he did an oil of a skeleton wrapped in translucent green skin, sunk up to its waist in muck in an endless tunnel. He called the painting, *Man in Woman's Womb.*

In one of his drawings, he turned a man into an ashtray. From a round base, the torso, a long neck rises to support a head, pierced through, Dali-like, by a mouth smoking a cigar. The hand of one long tubelike arm helps hold the cigar. The hand of the other arm holds a spray of lighted cigarettes.

Perhaps this drawing was partially responsible for Kenneth Anger's assertion, in *Hollywood Babylon*, that Jimmy dug "sex assorted with beatings, boots, belts and bondage—*spiced with knowing cigaret burns* (which gave Jimmy his underground nickname: The Human Ashtray) . . ."

One morning, in the dim of dawn, Bill opened his eyes to check the alarm clock. In its place he saw what he slowly realized was a life-size green clay cross section of a woman's pelvis, inverted so that the vagina served as holder for a huge white candle that was burning brightly, dripping hot wax over the thighs. Jimmy had stayed up all night, sculpturing this newest masterpiece. Now he was standing near the bed, laughing, enjoying its effect on his half-awake roommate.

In the common cause of meeting the rent and utility bills (they sometimes had dinner by candlelight—"Lightless Fridays"—to save electricity) Jimmy and Bill helped each other as much as they could. Jimmy introduced Bill to Isabelle Draesmer and Bill got Jimmy a job as a part-time usher at CBS. But Jimmy was fired at the end of his first week because he couldn't help smirking when the head usher issued instructions. He couldn't manage to look neat in the uniform, either. Much to the distress of his superiors, he called it "the monkey suit."

The most helpful thing that Bill did for Jimmy was to introduce him to James Whitmore, a thirty-year-old actor whom Bill met at an audition in Hollywood. Whitmore had studied at the American Theatre Wing, at the Actors Studio, had appeared in *Command Decision* on Broadway and had come to the coast to play an important role in the movie *Battleground* for which, later, he would win an Oscar nomination as best supporting actor.

Whitmore was married and two of his three sons had been born at that time. He thought Los Angeles a better place than New York to raise his children and he liked the fact that Hollywood was beginning to provide him with more or less regular work. He did, however, miss the stimulation of New York theatre and the chance to experiment with other performers at the Actors Studio. So when several UCLA Theatre Arts students, including Bill Bast, asked him to lead an acting group, he agreed, provided no money change hands, because, he modestly insisted, he really knew nothing about acting, and even less about teaching it.

A room was found in the Brentwood Mart, and the group began to meet one evening a week. Jimmy attended these sessions regularly, but he began to cut more and more of his UCLA classes. Most days he went up to Hollywood to audition for TV and movie parts. The one thing that did still interest him at UCLA was getting into one of the Theatre Arts productions in Royce Hall.

Competition was tough. Casting resembled an old-time studio cattle call. There were long lines. In one of them, Jimmy and a friend, Joe Brown, who would later play Angel Obregon in *Giant*, waited their turn to go up on the great stage and read the mimeographed bits that had been handed out.

The spring play was *Dark of the Moon* by Howard Richardson and William Berney. Both Joe and Jimmy wanted the role of the Witch Boy who, upon seeing the beautiful Barbara Allen, whose ballad is sung in so many versions, falls in love and is given human form to marry her. But there is a catch. He can stay human only as long as she stays faithful.

If an actor made it through the general audition, his or her name would appear on the callback sheet the next day. The director, Edward Hearn, apparently thought that both Joe and Jimmy showed Witch Boy potential. Both their names showed up on the sheet next day. Joe remembers that "Jimmy was always pretty cool about callbacks. You knew he gave a damn but he was always kind of a loner."

In one of the GI barracks that had been thrown up behind Royce Hall to accommodate the influx of returning World War II veterans, Jimmy and Joe did further readings for director Hearn. By the last day, there were only three actors in the running: Jimmy, Joe, and a boy who was considerably taller than either of them. "The fact that the character was supernatural," says Joe, "didn't mean that he had to be big, tall or strong. I thought the character should move well—and, by the way, Jimmy moved beautifully, a little round-shouldered at times, but that wasn't pronounced then, not until later when I saw him after the Actors Studio experience. Then he came back kind of Brando-ish, but, of course, everybody was doing it in those days. Everybody became suddenly influenced by the new, quote, method. But at that time, he wasn't that way, he just tended to be a little round-shouldered. But for this part, the Witch Boy, I remember he straightened out. And his speech was absolutely clear. That was one of the things I noticed after I saw him, after so many years, when we worked together on *Giant*—his speech. I remember, I felt like telling him, Oh, come off it! Where are you getting that pattern of speech? But I never did. He was in a different league then. That was the biggest change I saw, because, you know, he wanted to do *Macbeth, Hamlet*, all of Shakespeare, and you can't do that with marbles in your mouth.

"Anyway, when we read for *Dark of the Moon*, he straightened out, all five feet eight inches of him, and he raised his head high. Hearn was in the back, and there were some other students there, and he began, and with that voice of his—it was that scene, they come in and accuse him of being a devil and he discovers that his baby is dead—and the lines were: 'I've lost my baby. My baby is dead. I've lost my baby.' And he built that, you know, until it just shook that damn building. I felt chills. The back of my hair stood up. The intensity! He really felt it, you know, physically. And that is something with young actors you just don't see. They may be all emotionally involved and intellectually involved, but physically they're not involved. But Jimmy's whole body, his whole soul was there. And when he read like that everybody applauded. And I had already read, and he'd said to me, 'Joe, you've got it.' And then, after he read, I said, 'Listen, baby, I *know* you got it.' And he said, 'You really think so?' At times he had an almost childlike quality, very sin-

cere, not mannered. But anyway, he didn't get the part
and I didn't get the part. The tall guy got it. And, you
know, when you don't get a part, you and the other people get together and discuss why you didn't get it, and
you try to be objective. But Jimmy, after losing that part,
just kind of clammed up and had nothing to do with anybody. I knew he was angry, heartsick about it. And then
he just kind of took off."

So far, the bright new year (1951) had proved a disaster: Jimmy had lost his job at CBS, been beaten out of
a part he wanted very badly, spent all his Pepsi commercial earnings on résumés and photographs, been forced,
finally, to borrow pocket money from Bill (who hardly
had any to lend) and now the rent was due again and
he didn't know where his half was coming from.

But one morning a Jerry Fairbanks producer called
to tell Jimmy that he had been cast as John the Baptist in
Hill Number One, a television drama he had auditioned
for several weeks earlier. It was scheduled for Easter release.

At first, Jimmy was thrilled. Then he plunged into a
depression, deeper than the one he had been in before
the good news. It was obvious to Bill that Jimmy was
afraid he wouldn't be able to carry off the role, but Jimmy
refused to talk about it. He seemed suddenly to have become superstitious as though mere mention of the project
would send the whole thing up in smoke. Worse, Bill suspected, Jimmy was hoarding his excitement, keeping it
all to himself.

At a meeting of the acting group that took place a

few days before Jimmy went into rehearsal for *Hill Number One*, Whitmore interrupted the ordinary exercises and asked for improvisations. Ironically, he paired Jimmy and Bill, who, by that time, had stopped speaking to each other.

He took Jimmy aside and told him that he was a college student who had stolen a watch. Later, he had taken the watch to a jeweler to have it repaired. But then he discovers that the cops are onto him. Now, it is his task to go back into the shop and get the watch away from the jeweler so he can get out of town on a bus leaving in fifteen minutes.

Then, out of Jimmy's hearing, Whitmore told Bill that he was a jeweler whom the police had telephoned about a thief of Jimmy's description. He remembers that a young man suiting that description had brought a watch in for repair a day or so earlier. If the young man returns, the jeweler's task is to stall, call the police and keep the suspect in his shop until a patrol car arrives.

The tension that had been building up between the two roommates should have made the improvisation explosive. Instead, their scene was dull and unconvincing. Jimmy exaggerated the craftiness of the thief to vaudeville proportions. Bill retreated to the purely rational aspects of the jeweler's character and quickly ran out of reasons to keep Jimmy in the shop. Whitmore stopped the show.

"It wasn't working," says Whitmore, "because it wasn't important enough to either of them. I don't remember exactly what happened, but I remember that it just kind of flattened out. I think Jimmy came in and said, 'I want the watch.' And Bill said, 'You can't have it.' And Jimmy said, 'Okay.' I mean, I'm exaggerating, there was a lot of talk in between, but basically, that was it. The thing you do in an instance like that is to say to a person, 'Find something that's meaningful to you, to you as a person.' And that will vary with the person, that something that really means something—your wife, your children, or whatever—but when you've got it, you've got a scene because it'll be important to you and hence to the audience."

Jimmy seemed to understand exactly what Whitmore was saying. This time he prepared the scene in deep concentration. Whitmore gave the signal to begin. Jimmy came on with an icy ferocity that really frightened his acting partner. Bill wanted to give up without a word. Then he remembered what he was supposed to do. He refused to hand over the watch. Jimmy got more and more demanding. Bill got more and more stubborn. Jimmy started calling Bill names—"Nickel-Nurser! Pompous bastard!"—using intimate information that really hurt. The jeweler began to tremble. "Why, you near-sighted little son-of-a-bitch!" he screamed, in a genuine rage. Jimmy grabbed Bill and hit him. Whitmore and the other members of the class jumped in and pulled the two actors apart.

When Jimmy got his breath again, he realized that he had experienced something new. Acting was Doing. It wasn't enough to understand all the various techniques of mind and body manipulation. Everything had to be welded into action. He had concentrated so hard he had gotten beyond just imitating the character. He had become the character. That's what it really meant to act. Now he was sure he could give a good performance in *Hill Number One.*

The shooting went well and Jimmy collected his first substantial acting fee. Most of it went for rent and gasoline. Soon he was broke again. Sometimes, when there wasn't even money for food, Jimmy would come up with weird emergency rations like dry oatmeal mixed with mayonnaise. For dessert, more oatmeal, but mixed with jam. Going around half-starved all the time did nothing to improve his mood, or Bill's.

Jimmy tried to get another acting job. Every morning he would climb into the fourthhand 1939 Chevy his father had bought him and drive up to Hollywood to make the rounds. But at that moment, for Jimmy Dean, there were no acting jobs.

He started going out late at night, taking long, lonely walks. He would go down to Venice's Pacific Ocean Park, an amusement pier that has since been boarded up and partially torn down. He would hang around the hotdog and clam stands, watch people eat, eavesdrop on drunks mumbling their troubles to indifferent strollers, kid around with the small-time gamblers and pimps who worked the beach front. Often, he finished off the night with a cup of coffee and a conversation with a tired counter girl. Then he would go back to the penthouse and collapse into bed, too worn out to worry about the chaos in his psyche or his struggle with the world.

Bill's mother came for a short visit, stuffed the refrigerator, cooked big meals. Her presence in the penthouse disturbed Jimmy—he once spent a whole day building a mobile without saying a word to her. But on Mother's Day he ran out, bought a box of candy and gave it to her with a picture of himself on which he wrote: "To my second mother, love, Jimmy."

A few days after Bill's mother left, the refrigerator was empty again. Jimmy looked harder for parts. Bill stuck to his underpaid usher's post at CBS. One day, in the corridor, he met Beverly Wills, who was playing Fluffy Adams on a big network comedy, "Junior Miss." Beverly and her mother, comedienne Joan Davis, lived in a Bel Air mansion with tennis courts, pool, bathhouse, and bar.

Bill and Jimmy began to hang out at Beverly's, free-loading food and drinks, swimming, dancing, sunning, listening to records. Sometimes, when Bill and Jimmy could scrape up a little money, they would double-date: Bill and Beverly, Jimmy and one of Beverly's friends.

One night, as Bill and Jimmy and Beverly were cruising around Hollywood in Jimmy's old Chevy, Beverly turned to Bill and announced that she and Jimmy were in love. Several times, she reminded him, when he'd worked late at CBS, he'd sent Jimmy over to pick her up. So she and Jimmy had been thrown together and one thing led to another—but couldn't they all stay friends because that was more important than anything.

Bill was stunned. He tried to tell himself that he had never really been serious about Beverly, that she and

Jimmy probably had a lot more in common than he and Beverly ever had and that it probably served him right —hadn't he been using her for drinks and dinners and pool parties?

But after Beverly had been dropped off in Bel Air, Jimmy calmly proceeded to betray her by promising Bill he would drop her flat if Bill were really interested. Bill was too concerned with keeping up a "manly" front to show any feeling for Beverly. After all, she was only a "chick." He swore that she had never really meant anything to him.

Next morning, still trying to keep up the uncomfortable pretense of being friends, the three drove out to Van Nuys where Jimmy was scheduled to appear in traffic court. Before he had been given a car of his own, he had borrowed his father's to move his stuff down to the Santa Monica penthouse. Coming back, he had managed to get a ticket for speeding. The first few notices found their way into the wastebasket, but the latest one had raised the fine from $10.00 to $25.00 and warned that a warrant for Jimmy's arrest would be issued if he didn't pay up or show up.

The man whose case preceded Jimmy's was accused of being a Peeping Tom. The judge dealt with him severely. Jimmy was terrified. When he got up to speak, his voice was so faint he could hardly be heard. "Your honor," he began, "I know I have done wrong by not taking care of this ticket before now, but I was afraid. Yes, sir. You see, I'm a student at UCLA. I've been having a rough time of it. I mean with money. I don't have much and what I do have goes mostly for food and books. I know twenty-five dollars doesn't sound like much to you, your honor, but to me it could mean food for a whole month or books for a whole semester."

An almost benign expression had appeared on the judge's face.

"I never would have done it, your honor," continued Jimmy, speaking louder, exploiting his success, "if I hadn't promised my father I'd have the car back that afternoon at five. He let me borrow it so I could go to an interview for a part-time job I needed. I guess I just didn't want to let my father down." His voice trailed off. He bowed his head, apparently too ashamed to go on.

"Five dollars," said the judge, banging his gavel.

As Jimmy paid his fine to the bailiff, he winked at Bill and Beverly across the courtroom and they had to make a dash for the doors so they wouldn't burst out laughing in front of the judge. In the parking lot, they complimented Jimmy on his flawless performance.

At Easter, when *Hill Number One* appeared on TV, Jimmy got more compliments for his acting, this time in newspapers and trade journals. Unfortunately, the offers he had expected to come flooding in after his first good reviews did not materialize.

Isabelle Draesmer called, but it was to tell him that a group of girls from Immaculate Heart High had formed a James Dean fan club. The telecast, it seemed, had been required viewing in one of their religion courses and they had really freaked out over John the Baptist. Now, they wanted to see him in person. They were giving a big party in his honor. Would he please come?

Jimmy took Bill along for company. They expected, with all their insecure collegiate superiority, to find themselves at a real kindergarten gathering. But the minute Jimmy walked through the door, he was mobbed by beautiful girls. They pressed around him, eating him up with their eyes, giggling, reaching out to touch him. He was confused for a moment, but quickly adjusted to his new glory. He began behaving like a star, flashing his blue eyes, smiling knowing smiles at the girls he found most attractive, delegating the less fortunate to "my good friend, Bill."

But the fan-club triumph didn't leave the two roommates any richer. When they were going over the household budget a few days later, Jimmy suggested that Bill hit some of his pals for a loan. Bill, who had already borrowed his way out of several friendships, wondered why Jimmy didn't put the bite on some of his own buddies. Was Bill really after the money he had been lending Jimmy? Jimmy chose to read it that way. Well, he was going to pay Bill back, every goddamned penny! But Jimmy knew what Bill was really pissed off about. What? What had happened with Beverly, that's what!

Other people were finding it just as hard to get along with Jimmy. One of them was Joan Davis. On the golf course with Beverly and Joan, Jimmy would often make comments on Joan's game. He would volunteer suggestions just before a particularly tough shot, when he knew the psychological sabotage would be greatest. Joan began to loathe him.

But Beverly still found him fascinating. When it came time for her birthday party, an important event for the movie capital's teen screen crowd, she invited Jimmy to be her date and even put ex-beau Bill Bast on the guest list. That year, the invited included Debbie Reynolds, who had just hit in MGM's *Three Little Words,* and Lugene Saunders, a television starlet who has since faded from the film firmament.

Also among the favored few was that year's All-America Archery champion, whom Beverly and Jimmy had met on a Hollywood target range. When the party was well under way and some of the guests were under the weather, Beverly and Jimmy asked Joan to take part in an impromptu archery exhibition. She gagged it up, pretended to be scared to death (as she probably was), but finally agreed. The bowman stood her in front of a big tree, handed her a bright pink balloon, told her to hold it out at arm's length. He drew back his bow string and fired. First arrow, Zing! Into the tree trunk. Second arrow, Zing! Into the trunk again. Obviously, the great marksman was just kidding around, building suspense. Joan was trembling. Zing! Bam! Balloon's eye with the third arrow. The circle of onlookers let out a great sigh of relief and clapped.

Then, to everyone's surprise, even Beverly's, Jimmy Dean stepped forward, brandishing a shiny red apple. He popped it on his head and proclaimed it the next target. With considerably less trepidation than the legendary

William Tell, the archer fitted another arrow into his bow, drew back the string, took careful aim and was about to let fly, when Joan Davis dashed forward and stopped the show. There was to be no stupid slaughter on her lawn. She could do without her share of Hollywood scandal.

Stymied, upstaged, outdone, Jimmy looked his own arrows at Miss Davis. She, for once having succeeded in squelching her daughter's upstart swain, left the field sporting a victor's smile.

One evening, not long after Beverly's party, Jimmy subjected Bill to three or four hours of one of his nastier moods and Bill decided to do some night prowling himself. He walked down to the palisades, looked out over the Pacific. He was getting to the end of his tolerance for Jimmy's aggressive gloom, his winner-take-all, cutthroat competitiveness. And there was no point in trying to talk things out with Jimmy. But Bill knew he had to talk to someone. Then he remembered that Jeanetta Lewis, a former UCLA Theatre Arts major, had rented an apartment a few blocks from the penthouse.

Jeanetta's lights were on. Bill knocked. She was glad to see him. She listened sympathetically to his account of the increasingly impossible Jimmy situation. When he got to the part about Jimmy making a pass at Beverly Wills behind his back, she exploded: "That two-timing little weasel!"

Bill was surprised and flattered by the intensity of Jeanetta's compassion. He understood better when she told him that Jimmy had been keeping her on the back burner all those months, telephoning, dropping by occasionally, making sure the flame didn't go out entirely. Bill was doubly disgusted.

Before he left, she told him that she was moving up to Hollywood the very next day to an apartment nearer her job. Would he give her a hand? He said he would.

In the morning, early, Jeanetta appeared at the penthouse. She tiptoed into the room where Jimmy was sleeping and pulled a big glossy photo out of his mirror frame. It showed her and Jimmy dancing at a Sigma Nu party. Whispering curses, she tore up the photograph so that the pieces fell over Jimmy's sleeping form. He would wake up to find himself covered with their mutilated images. It was primitive and satisfying.

Then she took Bill to breakfast. He was an idiot, she told him, not to walk out on a person like Jimmy. Bill agreed. She had an idea. Since they were moving her things up to Hollywood, why didn't they look around for a new place for him at the same time? Her fury forged his decision. That afternoon, they found him a new apartment, and he telephoned the penthouse landlady to tell her he was moving out immediately.

When he and Jeanetta got back to Santa Monica, Jimmy was waiting for them. He ran down the steps and took his stand on the lawn. As Bill approached, Jimmy threw down his glasses and grabbed him: "You son-of-a-bitch," he screamed, tears burning in his eyes, "you dirty son-of-a-bitch."

Jeanetta ran up, tugged at Jimmy's sleeve and began shouting: Why not hit her? She couldn't defend herself.

Wasn't it his style to hit people who couldn't defend themselves?

Jimmy told her to get the hell away. She pushed in closer. He hit her across the mouth, hard. She wobbled backward, almost fell, then moved in again, screaming: "Come on, Jimmy, why don't you hit me again?" And Jimmy did hit her again, twice, each time harder than the last, and blood spurted out of her lips. That stopped him cold. (A few years later, in *East of Eden,* he would play an almost exactly similar scene with Julie Harris and Dick Davalos.)

Bill steered Jimmy and Jeanetta up the stairs to the penthouse. Jeanetta retreated into the bathroom and vomited, wailing and moaning between heaves. Bill went into his bedroom to pack. When Jeanetta came out of the bathroom, Jimmy begged her to forgive him, got her aspirin, tissues, offered to make hot tea, apologized nonstop until Bill had taken his last bag out to the car. Then Jimmy began to cry. He held out his paw like a whipped dog. Bill couldn't bring himself to shake it. He figured Jimmy was putting on a sob show like the one he had done for the judge in Van Nuys. He turned and fled down the stairs.

SIX

The UCLA fall term was about to begin, but a few days after Bill Bast left the Santa Monica penthouse, Jimmy moved up to Hollywood, too. To hell with college. It wasn't getting him anywhere. He would put all his energy into acting. He became a pioneer dropout.

For the first few weeks he stayed with Ted Avery, an usher whom he had met during his whirlwind stint at CBS. Ted's wife was out of town visiting relatives. He invited Jimmy to share his apartment until she returned. And Jimmy needed work as well as a bed, so Ted, who had recently given up his job as a people parker at the studio to become a car parker in the lot next door, talked the manager into hiring his friend.

In addition to being an expert car jockey, Avery was an experienced cowpoke, and occasionally he would land a bit part in a Western. Since Jimmy wanted to be ready for any role that might come his way, he begged Ted to teach him to ride and rope. Sometimes, after their sessions in the saddle, they would clown around the

CBS lobby in full western gear, much to the distress of the worshipful tourists who had traveled so far to visit the temple of the radio gods.

More often than not, life at the parking lot was misery. Almost all of the attendants were out-of-work actors. Nobody had any money. Sometimes, Jimmy would ask one of the other men to cover him for a two-hour audition and be gone for days. Sometimes he slept in his old Chevy, because he didn't have rent for a room. Sometimes, when he didn't have money for food, he accepted dinner invitations from obviously gay men. If anyone kidded him about these "dates," he would laugh and dismiss them as "free meal tickets." But his agent, Isabelle Draesmer, had seen this particular show-business scene played out too many times to be confused about what was really going on. "It was a question," she says, "of marrying Joan Davis' daughter or going off to live with a studio director."

Jimmy soon found a way to dump Beverly. The William Tell incident at her birthday party had established him as persona non grata number one at the Bel Air house. He and Beverly met instead at Paradise Cove, a slightly sleazy fun spot on the Pacific Coast Highway near Malibu, where her father maintained a weekend getaway trailer. Beverly loved the big-band dances at the Paradise Pavilion. Jimmy didn't. For all his athletic skill, he wasn't as good a dancer as Beverly and sometimes, she just couldn't resist picking out a young man who could match her, step for step. The resulting exhibitions made Jimmy feel more than a little left out, and since now he

94

really wanted out, one night, just as Beverly was slipping into the arms of a more nimble partner, Jimmy stomped out of her life forever.

"He said we could have twin beds," Jimmy told Isabelle Draesmer, concerning the offer made to him by Rogers Brackett, a CBS television director who was to pluck Jimmy out of the parking lot and begin promoting his career. "The next thing," says agent Draesmer, "they were living together; and it was with this man he went to Chicago—and on to New York."

Rogers Brackett had come to the coast from New York, where he had been a television producer with Grey Advertising. His colleagues at the agency had long suspected that he was more deeply committed to theatre, ballet, and cinema than he was to the dreary Punch-and-Judy television commercials he went through the motions of making for his bi-weekly pay check.

The move into Rogers' comfortable quarters on Sunset Plaza Drive, a steep road that snakes its way up into the Hollywood Hills from Sunset Strip, gave Jimmy a taste of luxury he had never known before. It was exhilarating to live high up in a city that put so many people down. Looking out over a panorama that swept all the way from city hall's gray tower to the blur of white yachts in the Marina Del Rey gave one an exhilarating sense of power. By night, the basin was a magic carpet of colored light. Even on smoggy days, when the view was gone, a sense of superiority remained. The hill dweller breathed cleaner air than the millions of unseen automobile ants suffocating down there under that filthy orange cloud.

Rogers changed Jimmy's life professionally, too. He got him several bit parts on CBS radio shows like "Stars over Hollywood" and "Alias Jane Doe." Soon, Jimmy landed a film bit at Paramount: three lines in a Dean Martin and Jerry Lewis comedy, *Sailor Beware*. The lines ended up in a cutting-room barrel, but Jimmy himself stayed in— a smiling, well-scrubbed gob in the background of several scenes. Not long after that, he soldiered briefly in Samuel Fuller's *Fixed Bayonets* at Twentieth Century-Fox. In the background again, but covered with mud this time, he was a war-torn GI doling out death to "little yellow men" in Korea. After that, in *Somebody Stole My Gal*, a Universal-International musical starring Rock Hudson and Piper Laurie, Jimmy went back to being the toothy teen-ager of the Pepsi-Cola commercial, except that this time his adolescent cravings were fixed on oversized banana splits and cherry-topped chocolate fudge sundaes. A few frames of his "big" scene, with Charles Coburn, actually made the distribution prints.

While trying to make his way as an actor, Jimmy had traded the naïve, pet-and-fret world of college students for the hard-core, play-it-for-keeps struggle of Hollywood hopefuls, hookers, and hustlers. In between film and radio bits, he often night-owled at a gay meat rack on Hollywood Boulevard, a small club just east of the Hollywood Freeway. For a while, it seemed to him that he had landed smack in the middle of the real making-it milieu. Everybody talked a great game of acting and art. It took him some time to realize that he was doggy-paddling in a backwater of name-droppers, star-fuckers, leather freaks, drag queens—no-talents, for the most part, who put on their best performances in bars and beds.

Oral history at some of the leather-and-chain bars on the New York waterfront holds that Jimmy did some hustling himself during the early Hollywood days, that he was, in fact, an "instant hit with the fist-fuck set" because he would do things no one else dared to do.

Is there truth in such stories or do they merely recount the apocryphal adventures of a cult hero? Whatever the case, Jimmy would hardly be the first young actor who found himself forced to climb the ladder of success pants down. Exaction of sexual dues by those in power is an honored Hollywood tradition and it includes both sexes, whether hetero, homo, or anywhere in between.

One famous studio tyrant, who earned the scary sobriquet "White Fang," was reputed to put each would-be starlet through his own sadistic "screen test." The trap was, of course, baited with the offer of a contract which would turn out to be as phony as the diamond the poor girl would be promised for her very own, if, at the climax of her obscene ordeal, she could manage to tongue it out of its curious setting.

And there are even darker tales of young lovelies (and young studs) who, because they refused to stay fucked and forgotten, got dumped dead into the seaweedy waves at Malibu or tossed across the back fence of a rival studio lot to turn up days later as an embarrassing corpse not called for in the script.

Jimmy knew the fame game was dangerous, and at

times he sought relief from it by having dinner with his ex-roommate, Bill Bast, who was still going to UCLA. They had run into each other at several casting calls and soon they were back on speaking terms. Usually, Jimmy was able to keep up a façade of self-confidence, only slightly shivered by irony. But one night, at a little restaurant called the Tam O'Shanter, he broke into an impassioned tirade: Trying to get ahead in Hollywood was like living in Rome under Caligula. That's what the power people were like. They would give you some disgusting, humiliating task to perform and then punish you as an unworthy person for doing something so degrading. Of course, if you didn't follow orders, you were beheaded for disobedience. It was horrible that they had all those poor kids running after them, sucking around, turning somersaults, killing themselves to get into their good graces, only to be rewarded with a swift kick in the ass.

Jimmy confessed that he had "done a little dancing" himself and he had found out it didn't pay off. Well, he almost shouted, if he couldn't make it on his talent, he didn't want to make it at all. He might never get a chance to work in goddamned Hollywood, but at least the bastards would respect him.

A few days after the Tam O'Shanter dinner, Jimmy went to James Whitmore for advice. Through the torrent of painful personal problems Whitmore heard the young man saying that he really wanted to become an actor. "You'll have to go to New York," he told Jimmy. "Wherever the theatre is, that's where you learn your craft. People approach acting differently in New York."

The talk with Whitmore confirmed what Rogers Brackett and many other friends had told Jimmy. Even the drifters at Schwab's admitted that the only place to become a real actor was New York. The theatre was there. Live television was booming there. And above all, the Actors Studio was there.

While Jimmy was thinking all this over, Rogers got a directing assignment in Chicago and another in New York. Jimmy seemed to take the news calmly, but a few days before Rogers' departure, Mrs. Brackett, Rogers' mother, found Jimmy sobbing his heart out in the bathroom. When she told Rogers about it, he realized that Jimmy was terrified at the idea of being left behind. He arranged to take Jimmy along.

In Chicago, Rogers soon noticed that Jimmy was going crazy with boredom and decided to ship him ahead to New York. He called a friend, composer Alec Wilder, who lived at the Algonquin, and asked him to get Jimmy a room at the Iroquois, a hotel a few doors down the street. "Well," remembers Wilder, "Jimmy started to fabricate his own sources. It was kind of amusing. He came in a compartment on the Twentieth Century at Rogers' expense, of course, and burst into the Algonquin dining room and ate a very large and expensive breakfast. Immediately started to tell me some silly story, I don't remember what it was, to throw me off. I was a stranger and he was going to show me that he was the wild young man. It was some nutty story about a fire in Chicago, something like that. And I knew that Rogers called him Hamlet, that was his name for him, and Rogers

99

knew about his fix on acting. Anyway, I got him the room and he was hanging around, doing nothing, sitting on the bellboys' bench at the Algonquin most of the time. Somewhere along the way, he bought himself a recorder. I used to write little tunes for him and he called me and tried to play them back over the phone."

"New York overwhelmed me," Jimmy said later. "For the first few weeks I was so confused that I strayed only a couple of blocks from my hotel off Times Square. I would see three movies a day in an attempt to escape from my loneliness and depression. I spent over one hundred and fifty dollars of my limited funds on seeing movies."

When Rogers arrived, Jimmy began to get his courage back. He called some of the telephone numbers he had collected on the coast. James Sheldon, an NBC director, had no immediate assignments open but was sufficiently taken with Jimmy's good looks and his good audition to send him over to Jane Deacy, who was working in the Louis Shurr agency.

This remarkable woman, who now concerns herself exclusively with the career of George C. Scott, began her own career as a switchboard operator at Louis Shurr. By the time Jimmy came slouching in to see her, she had become an agent and was even thinking about opening her own agency. Like Adeline Nall in Fairmount and Gene Owen in Santa Monica, she knew at first sight that she was looking at and (when the boy finally did get around to speaking) listening to an exceptional human being.

Other talent agents, like Peter Witt, who often saw Jimmy sitting at the counter of NBC's Cromwell Drugstore (the East Coast equivalent of Schwab's), were kind enough to whisper a casting tip in Jimmy's ear from time to time (Witt helped Jimmy into his first Broadway show, *See the Jaguar*), but they never thought of signing him.

Jane Deacy signed him immediately and got right to work on his career. His first job wasn't even on camera. He was hired as a standby comic on a CBS Saturday night TV show called "Beat the Clock." The format called for the contestants to act out, spontaneously, various sight and situation gags. It was Jimmy's job to rehearse the "absolutely unprepared and unrehearsed" contestants for these funny bits.

He proved to be an expert clown coach. His sense of the absurd, not to say of the silly, was highly developed. He could open himself up to the zaniest nonsense and act it into reality without the slightest embarrassment. Soon the director let him loose on whole audiences. He became the show's warm-up man.

Television was exciting in the early fifties. The New York networks were giving the Hollywood studios a run for their profits. Later, both would decide that it was better business to cool the competition, and by 1957, when tape came in, the tube's great cultural revolution was definitely over.

But on a typical week in 1953 (April 1 to 7), there were over thirty shows that kept their cameras pointed at live actors. Among them: "Broadway TV Theatre," "Hall of Fame Theatre," "Robert Montgomery Presents,"

"Studio One," "Star Theatre," "Fireside Theatre," "Circle Theatre," "NBC Television Theatre," "Four Star Playhouse," "Video Theatre," "Playhouse of Stars." There were live mysteries, live comedies, and a great live satire—Sid Caesar's "Show of Shows."

Soon Jane Deacy was able to get Jimmy some work in front of the camera. He got a walk-on in a "Studio One" production. He did bits on "Treasury Men in Action," "Tales of Tomorrow," "The Web," "Martin Kane," "Kraft Theatre," "Danger." In a radio play, *The Thief*, on "Theatre Guild of the Air," Jane even managed to get him a lead.

A few weeks after Rogers Brackett arrived in New York, he found a studio atop a five-story loft building in the West Twenties, and Jimmy moved in with him as planned, but he also began seeing a young woman named Dizzy Sheridan. Dizzy, the daughter of a pianist named Frank Sheridan, wanted to be a dancer. To support herself while she studied, she worked as an usher at the Paris Cinema on Fifty-eighth Street. Her battle for artistic success was just as painful as Jimmy's. Knowing her took some of the hard edge off the competition that was constantly bearing down on him in the big, brutal city. And Dizzy was someone to whom he could confess his confusion about his homosexual affairs; her experience in the dance world had made her thoroughly familiar with the life style Jimmy described.

When, a few months later, Bill Bast, who was looking for a job in a Madison Avenue ad agency, showed up in New York, he and Jimmy decided to try rooming together again. Jimmy moved out of Rogers Brackett's studio. He and Bill found a ninety-a-month double at the Hotel Iroquois.

One morning, not long after moving back to the Iroquois, Jimmy stopped in at Jane Deacy's office to find a thin blond girl in a red dress tapping away at the office typewriter. He slipped up beside her and peered over her shoulder. When she looked up, he asked her what she was doing. She told him to get lost.

Half an hour later she finished her typing. As she walked through the waiting room on her way out, she noticed that the smallish young man with glasses who had come on to her earlier was still there, sitting on the couch. Almost involuntarily, she stopped, swung around and, as if to return the challenge, asked him what his name was.

"Jimmy," said the young man indistinctly, and invited her to have a cup of coffee with him.

Eventually, she got around to telling him her name: Christine White. She also told him that she was an actress and that she had been working on an original scene up in Jane's office. Jimmy read the scene, a boy-and-girl beach encounter. He liked it. He and Christine decided to use it to try to get into the Actors Studio, hoping against hope that the combination of their talents and this original material would find favor with Strasberg and Kazan.

For the next five weeks, they rehearsed every day, working all over town—in Chris's apartment, in Jimmy's hotel room, in bars, cafeterias, in Central Park. The day of the audition finally came, windy and cold. When Jimmy and Chris got out of the elevator on the fourteenth floor of 1697 Broadway, Jimmy climbed onto a steaming radiator and stayed there until he thawed out. The place was full of scared actors waiting to go on in the shabby little auditorium at the end of the hall.

After a while, Chris got up and went over to Jimmy. Shouldn't they run the lines a last time? With a look of terror in his eyes, he muttered something about not wanting to run the lines and then, in a clearer voice, he said he wasn't going to do the scene at all.

Chris was stunned. After five weeks' work. To be betrayed now! And it was Jimmy who had talked her into doing her original scene instead of using *The Master Builder* as she intended. It was Jimmy who had insisted that they take the gamble together. It was Jimmy who had introduced her to his friends during the last weeks with: "We're working on a scene for the Actors Studio. It's a tough wall to crack, so meet my partner in crime." All this went screaming through her head.

Her hands grabbed at the bag in which they had brought their props for the scene: two cans of beer. She opened both cans, took one for herself, handed the other to Jimmy. His frozen face cracked open to take in beer. And then Chris got herself together enough to tell him that he was ruining her audition as well as his own. Did he know that? Did he understand what he was doing? Jimmy gulped more beer.

"Dean, Dean," they heard the secretary call out. They

had registered under Dean because "D" was nearer the top of the alphabet than "W" for White. Again: "Dean!" Jimmy threw his beer can to the floor, tromped on it, ran down the hall, into the stairwell. He was gone.

The secretary, who had observed, even if she had not understood, Jimmy's behavior, suggested to Chris that she put the audition under White to allow herself and her partner more time. Chris nodded and collapsed on a bench, eyes closed, wondering why she didn't pass out.

Time stopped dead. Then she felt something wet, cool, hard. Jimmy was standing in front of her, rolling an icy can of beer back and forth on her forehead (a gesture he was to repeat with a milk bottle on his own forehead in *Rebel Without a Cause*).

"Hello, Clayton," Jimmy said, using the name of the girl she was to play in the scene, "see you on the beach." He had run out to get more beer. He hadn't wanted to work with empty cans. Running up and down fourteen flights had exhausted his fear. He began hopping around, shadow-boxing, muttering to himself.

When, a few minutes later, the secretary called Chris's name, Jimmy dashed right out onto the stage, flopped down on the hard floor as though it really were sand, and popped open his can of beer. Without his glasses, he had misjudged the distance and landed far over to one side. Chris hesitated for a moment, then walked out and sat down in the center where they had planned to play the scene. Jimmy squinted to find her, caught sight of the bold white checks on her blouse, rolled toward her, and bobbed up alongside with a "Hi" that was not in the script. They plunged into the scene.

It went on for more than the allotted five minutes. When it ended—the boy invites the girl into his cabin but she runs off into the night, there was a silence. Then a voice said, "My name is Elia Kazan. This is Lee Strasberg and Cheryl Crawford. Who wrote the scene?"

Chris ran out onto the stage again. "I did."

"That's very nice," said Kazan. A new silence.

"Very, very sensitive," said Strasberg. More silence. Jimmy just stood there. Chris had to pull him off the stage.

That night, Jimmy, who almost never wrote letters, did write to Uncle Marcus and Aunt Ortense. "I have made great strides in my craft," he said. "After months of auditioning, I am very proud to announce that I am a member of the Actors Studio, the greatest school of the theatre." He explained that the school "housed" such famous people as Marlon Brando, Julie Harris, Arthur Kennedy, Elia Kazan, Mildred Dunnock, Kevin McCarthy, Montgomery Clift, and June Havoc. "If," he went on, "I can keep this up and nothing interferes with my progress, one of these days I might be able to contribute something to the world."

He asked his aunt and uncle to tell Adeline Nall that he had never forgotten the Thespian Creed: "Act well your part for there all honor lies."

He also asked if they could spare "10 dollars or so," and, after apologizing for asking at all, told them he would never forget what they had done for him. "I want to repay you," he said in closing, "It takes time and many disappointments. I'll try not to take too long."

Marcus and Ortense wrote back immediately, sending congratulations, love, and money.

SEVEN

Actors lead hard lives, especially in the early years. Break-ing through requires talent, indomitable drive, and a lot of luck.

Perhaps the worst of all acting career hazards is wait-ing: waiting to see agents; waiting to see directors; wait-ing to see producers; waiting outside a dressing room to congratulate someone who's just hit in a part you tried for and didn't get; waiting, when you do get a part, to go on; waiting, later, to see what the reviews say; waiting to see if you have an acting career at all.

If you flop, it's back to the agony of auditions, to the despair of long lines at the unemployment office. Most people can hardly bear even remembering the pain of losing a job or of looking for a new one. For an actor, being out of work is a way of life. Looking for a job is half the job.

If you hit, it seems sudden. Your friends think it hap-pened overnight. You remember all the hard work and still you know that getting a break had a great deal to do with your success. You wonder if you've really earned all that praise. You discover that you need more and more of it to convince yourself that you really did. You begin to feel guilt about the people you left behind to struggle on in obscurity.

No wonder so many stars behave obnoxiously. All the power and glamour in the Hollywood world don't seem enough to compensate for the deprivation, the humiliation endured on the way up. Even taking it out on others doesn't discharge all the accumulated rage.

Then, sometimes, fame and fortune disappear as quickly, as capriciously, as they came, and there is the awful readjustment to being just a plain person again, the terror of turning into a hopeless has-been.

After only a year in New York, Jimmy felt that he was starting to move. There were good signs. Directors began to treat him with more respect. Jane Deacy got inquiries about him from casting people. But even in the midst of the live television boom, he could not yet pick up enough parts to feed himself regularly.

Breakfast was often supplied by a coffee-shop waitress named Marie, who would serve Jimmy and Bill eggs and charge them only for toast and coffee. But that left lunch, dinner, and the room rent at the Iroquois, where the desk clerk couldn't write off their bill no matter how sorry he felt for the two good-looking young men.

He did, however, come up with some help. One day, when the photographer whose studio was just off the lobby happened to complain to him that a male model had failed to show up for work, he rang Jimmy and Bill's room. Soon, both were doing once-in-a-while ten-dollar-a-session posing assignments. Then Bill got a job in the CBS Press Relations Division. But as the months of spring passed, there were fewer and fewer acting bits for Jimmy and he could see that the modeling fees and Bill's exploit-the-apprentice salary at the network were never going to float them through the summer doldrums.

He followed up every lead. He tried to get an audition for a Mary Chase play, *Bernadine*, but Miss Chase left for Colorado before he could reach her. John Kerr got the role. He tried to get an audition for the Clarence Day Jr. part in a proposed CBS "Life with Father" series. The producers said they weren't ready to cast.

Rogers Brackett had been calling him again. He decided to accept an invitation to join Rogers for a weekend at Lemuel Ayres's house on the Hudson. Cool, clean country air was a relief after the city's dirty heat. At dinner, he heard conversation about Ayres's forthcoming production of a new N. Richard Nash play, *See the Jaguar*.

The Ayreses got to like Jimmy. They invited him back for several more weekends, with and without Rogers. He didn't push the relationship. He had learned from past toe-stubbings to be more subtle in his approach. Lem Ayres did not even find out that Jimmy was an actor until late in August when he and his wife invited him to be a member of the crew for a ten-day cruise on their sloop. During the sail-around, Jimmy found the proper time and place to let the producer know of his struggle for success as an actor. Ayres promised Jimmy he would give him a crack at a part in *Jaguar* when it went into production that fall.

Before leaving for the cruise, Jimmy had told Bill Bast he wouldn't have the money to pay his share of their Iroquois room rent for the time he would be away. Bill couldn't afford to keep the room by himself, so he moved into a summer sublet with a girl he knew from UCLA.

When Jimmy came back to the city, he moved in with Bill and the girl, but then the couple who had sublet the apartment, and who had supposedly gone away for the entire summer, returned unexpectedly and kicked all three of their young tenants out into the street.

The three decided that they would look for an apartment of their own, but at the same time they realized that, even combined, their earnings couldn't manage an average rent. Jimmy persuaded Dizzy Sheridan to make it a foursome. They found a big, shabby apartment in the West Eighties off Central Park West and moved in. Except for several old beds, the place was empty. There was no money for tables and chairs, sheets and pillow cases, pots and pans. Food was pretty scarce, too, most of the time.

One night, Martin Landau, an actor friend, invited Jimmy to dinner at his mother's house in Queens. Mrs. Landau stuffed Jimmy with food and, as he was leaving for home, pressed a large box into his hands.

When he got back to the Upper West Side apartment, his roommates were eager to know what the mysterious box contained. Leftovers, maybe? They hadn't been lucky enough to get an invitation to dinner. Without a word,

Jimmy carried the box into his bedroom. The roommates followed. He opened the box, drew out two blue sheets, a blue pillow case, a big blue pillow and a blue blanket. He proceeded to make up his bed, executing each tuck and fold with a flourish. When the work was perfect, he surveyed it, permitted himself a smile of satisfaction, dropped his pants and slid into his snug new nest.

Then, with no more explanation than he had offered them, the three roommates pulled the sheets out from under him, tumbled him to the floor and left him struggling to smother an attack of the giggles under a mound of twisted bedclothes. Jimmy loved to tease, but he could laugh even when one of his pranks was turned against him.

Horsing around burned up a lot of energy that, in those difficult months, could only have turned into anger. Jimmy seemed to understand that. He tried to keep busy. When he wasn't setting up a gag, he was working out as a parlor bullfighter. From Hollywood he had brought a toreador's cape and a set of bull horns, souvenirs of occasional weekend visits to Tijuana. He would talk one of his roommates into charging him with the horns and then whirl out of danger with a graceful twist of the cape.

The fall season had begun. Jimmy began to get TV bits again. Occasionally, too, he would take part in a play, even though the budget sometimes made no provision for paying the actors. Howard Sackler (who later wrote *The Great White Hope*) offered Jimmy a part in Ezra Pound's translation of Euripides' *Women of Trachis*, which he was directing at the New School. The play got

Jimmy little, if any, notice; but during rehearsals he met Leonard Rosenman, who had composed music for the show and who would later write scores for both *East of Eden* and *Rebel Without a Cause.*

Rosenman was only seven years older than Jimmy, but he was already an accomplished artist. He had studied with Schönberg. He had been composer in residence at Tanglewood. He had written important orchestral works. He was a fine pianist. Jimmy began to hang around him trying to siphon off all the musical culture he could. He even asked to be taken on as a piano pupil although he had never done even beginner's work at the keyboard. When Rosenman pointed that out, Jimmy only begged harder. Finally, the composer gave in.

But Jimmy never made much progress on the piano because he insisted on trying to learn show-off pieces that were far beyond his skill. When he heard Rosenman practicing an extraordinarily difficult Beethoven sonata (Opus 111), he decided that he must learn it, too. Rosenman tried to tell him that it would be folly to attempt the work because even he, Rosenman, who had studied piano since childhood, could hardly play it, and he doubted that even a virtuoso like Schnabel could do well with it. But Jimmy kept fumbling at the piece and never became convinced that he couldn't master it.

Jimmy often showed up for his lessons carrying impressive books (Kierkegaard, Huxley, Woolf), but later, in California, when Rosenman was working on Jimmy's first picture, he discovered that his friend had probably never read them. The two men were sitting on the beach at

Santa Barbara. The composer was reading a novel which director William Wyler had given him to see if he would like to score the movie version. When he had finished a hundred pages or so he looked up and noticed that Jimmy was still on the first three pages of the book he was reading. He saw, too, that Jimmy was pushing a finger along the lines of type and moving his lips. "Jimmy," he said, "I never noticed that before. Do you have a reading problem? Because, you know, that can be taken care of very easily." Jimmy stared at Rosenman savagely for a moment, and then exploded. When the composer got him to stop screaming and cursing, Jimmy, almost in tears, admitted that he did have a reading problem, that he had always had a reading problem. In high school he had been forced to work twice as hard as the other kids just to stay even.

By early October, roommates Jimmy and Dizzy and Bill were so broke that they had to split one bowl of chili three ways. Forking the last bean into his mouth, Jimmy mumbled something about taking a trip out to his uncle's farm in Indiana. He danced visions of Aunt Ortense's cooking before his famished roommates' eyes: steaks and roast beef, potatoes and pie. Within a few hours, they were on their way. A bus dropped them at the New Jersey Turnpike. They put out their thumbs. Two rides later (during one of which the driver made none-too-veiled suggestions about a motel foursome), they found themselves at the end of the Pennsylvania Turnpike.

It was about ten o'clock at night by then, dark and freezing cold. They were terribly hungry. The only place open was an ice cream stand. They ate several plates each and got back on the road. After what seemed an eternity, a Nash Rambler station wagon stopped and picked them up. The driver was a professional baseball player named Clyde McCullough on his way to an exhibition game in Des Moines. Clyde thought of himself as a performer. He had great sympathy for the misfortunes of the young dancer, the young actor, and the young writer. He made an impassioned speech about the stupidity of a nation which couldn't see the importance of subsidizing its artists. Then he himself subsidized his new friends' dinner and hours later, without a single obscene innuendo, dropped them off at an intersection a few miles north of Fairmount.

Dawn was just breaking, but early or late, announced or unannounced, Jimmy and Jimmy's friends were welcome at the Winslow farm. The three worn-out hitchhikers ate and bathed and went to bed. When they woke up, they ate some more. Jimmy talked farming with Uncle Marcus, told Aunt Ortense all about his acting career, played with his young cousin Markie Jr., showed off for Bill and Dizzy by doing stunts on his old Czech motorcycle. Getting off the bike afterward, he muttered something to his uncle: "Guess I'll never sell it. Like an old friend. Friends are hard to find in the theatre."

Next day, Jimmy took Dizzy and Bill into Fairmount to visit his high school drama teacher, Adeline Nall. She asked them to speak to her classes. Jimmy talked about acting, Dizzy talked about dancing, Bill talked about writing and directing. They enjoyed being the big shots from New York.

Then, just as they were beginning to stop worrying about where their next meal was coming from, Jane Deacy called from New York to say that Lemuel Ayres had asked her to send Jimmy over to read for a part in *See the Jaguar*. And it wasn't just a walk-on—it was a lead. Could he return immediately? Jimmy and Bill and Dizzy said reluctant good-byes to the Winslows and got out on the road again to hitch back to New York.

When Jimmy got back to the city two days later, he found out that another young actor had been doing the backers' auditions and was first in line for the role. His only hope would be to read so brilliantly that producer Ayres and director Michael Gordon would have no choice but to cast him.

The play, set at a gas station in "the nearby mountains of a western state," attempts primal passion and high poetry but falls somewhere in the limbo between *Tobacco Road* and *Desire Under the Elms*. In addition to a gas pump and a Coca-Cola cooler, the station boasts a curious zoo. "See the Ferret! See the Fox!" say signs intended to attract passing motorists. Brad, the station owner, dreams that one day he will trap a jaguar that has been seen in the forest. He has already prepared a large cage and painted a sign, "See the Jaguar!"

As the play advances, we learn that an old mountain woman, Mrs. Wilkins, keeps her son, Wally, a prisoner in an abandoned ice locker. However, before she dies, she sets him free with a rifle. After various adventures on the mountain with Janna, Brad's daughter, and Gramf, an old man who is clubbed to death by a mountaineer mob, the innocent, almost idiotic, Wally Wilkins shoots the jaguar. This so frustrates the gas station owner that he seizes the boy and throws him into the cage intended for the animal. When Dave, Janna's lover, comes to smash the locked cage, Wally doesn't even want out.

WALLY

I used to ask me Ma:
Let me out of the ice locker
So I can see the birds
And all the green things on the hill.
And she would say:
You wouldn't like out there,
Where people are . . .
Reckon she was right.

DAVE
(with desperate pity)

Don't you think it, boy!
Things will get better for you,
If I can get you out!

WALLY

Iffen you do get me out . . .
Can I go back to the ice locker?

Not an easy role. One misstep and the character becomes sentimental, or worse, silly. But Jimmy read Wally so convincingly that producer, director and playwright agreed the part should be his.

Rehearsals went well. In Arthur Kennedy, who was playing Brad, Jimmy found an actor he could respect. In Michael Gordon, he found a director more competent than the men he had worked for (and often fought with) in television. Mildred Dunnock, who had starred with Kennedy on Broadway in *Death of a Salesman* three years earlier, and who later would act with Jimmy in a television play, came to the opening at the Cort Theatre (December 3, 1952). "I'll never forget that," she says. "He was in a cage. Some of the lines were so unbelievable they were funny. And this drove Jimmy up the wall. He was very bright, with an absolute instinct. He could smell falseness, he could smell artificiality. He was like a streak of light.

"He was primarily a person who was trying to find himself, trying to find the truth through himself. I think one of the problems of The Method is that when you come upon it and it fascinates you, as it must have fascinated him, you become obsessed with certain doctrines, that is, *the simple truth*—it's better to be nothing, but be *truthful*. Well, this leads to a kind of purism and simplism that a theatrical person like Jimmy, because he was theatrical, he had *temperament*, could not—well, it caused an ambivalence in his nature. He was constantly at war with it, at war with the desire to be theatrical and the desire to be truthful. And since it was an era in The Method when anything that smacked of theatricality was squelched, unless it was a theatricality of nothing, that demanded a good deal."

At the opening night party at Sardi's, Jimmy got his first taste of Broadway star treatment. Suddenly he was somebody. People he didn't know pressed up to him and whispered awe-struck congratulations.

The morning papers also congratulated the actors, but condemned the play. "What started out," wrote Walter Kerr in the *Herald Tribune*, "as a surprisingly convincing evening ends as a disappointingly contrived one." Later in the review, Kerr said, "James Dean adds an extraordinary performance to an almost impossible role." The other critics sang pretty much the same song and the show folded in six days.

From the warm ashes of *Jaguar*, Jimmy's career began to rise. People (including producers, directors, agents, actors, angels and sponsors) began talking about James Dean. Columnists called Jane Deacy to see if they could interview her young client. MGM called, too, with an offer to send Jimmy to the coast for a screen test. Jane and Jimmy decided that it was not the moment for him to go to Hollywood. He would wait until he had a really big role under his belt before he put himself in a studio's power.

Jimmy had climbed to a new plateau. He was beginning to earn real money. Now he could afford to live alone and he decided to try it. He moved out of the apartment he shared with Dizzy and Bill and back into the Hotel Iroquois this time into a single room. And since, without Jimmy, Dizzy and Bill couldn't carry the rent, they were forced to move, too. Bill found a place to stay in a friend's apartment. Dizzy took a small room in Midtown.

Shortly after the move, Dizzy left New York for a dancing job in the Caribbean and Jimmy began seeing a lot of new girls. He would meet them at Jane Deacy's office, at one of the show-business drugstores, Walgreen's or Cromwell's, at one of the theatre bars, like Jerry's on Sixth Avenue and Fifty-fourth Street, or on the sidewalk outside. The relationship would last a few hours or a few days. Jimmy would take the girl to dinner, for a walk, to an interview, to an audition, on a wild cab ride, to a rehearsal, to Central Park Zoo, to bed, to breakfast, and then good-bye, see you later, subtext, never.

At the same time Jimmy was seeing a lot of actor Frank Corsaro, who had played in *Mrs. McThing* with Helen Hayes. Corsaro was a cultivated man who taught Jimmy a lot about art, about literature, about music, and about life.

This pattern became typical for Jimmy. He tried to keep people in communication-tight compartments. Certain people in his life had no idea that others, with whom he was equally intimate, even existed. He was also close-mouthed about his career. This discretion, this defensiveness, grew harder and harder to maintain as his acting brought him into the public eye.

In January, he got a good part in *Taken from the Hound of Heaven*, a Kate Smith dramatic presentation. In the following months, he got supporting roles in "Treasury Men in Action" and in "The Big Story," an

NBC series about newspapermen. As the year (1953) progressed, he got parts on "Armstrong Circle Theatre" (*The Bells of Cockaigne*), "Kraft Theatre," (*Keep Our Honor Bright*) and "Campbell Sound Stage" (*Life Sentence*). At the end of an appearance on the "Lux Video Theatre" he was honored with an interview. Then, in November, he got his first starring role, a lead opposite Naomi Reardon, in a Kraft Theatre play by Rod Serling, *A Long Time Until Dawn*.

Even though Marion Dougherty, who was casting for Kraft, had warned Dick Dunlap, the show's director, that Jimmy might be, as Dunlap puts it, an "undisciplined, really deep Studio type," he was shocked when Jimmy showed up late, rumpled, and dirty.

As soon as Dunlap could get to a phone he called Dougherty and said: "He was late, and if he's late again forget it, get somebody else." Dougherty said she would find a stand-by immediately and asked Dunlap to send Jimmy over to her office after rehearsal.

When Jimmy arrived she sat him down and gave him a polite, but firm, talking-to: Didn't he realize that this part could be a really important step in his career? He was just plain crazy if he didn't! But whatever he understood or didn't understand, he was going to "shape up or get shipped out."

At this point she looked across her desk and saw that Jimmy had fallen asleep. She could hardly believe her eyes. No one had ever pulled a stunt like that on her. She began to laugh. Jimmy woke up. She stopped laughing, gave him a final warning, and dismissed him.

Next day Jimmy showed up at the rehearsal hall on time. And he was clean. He eyed his stand-by, who had arrived early, with a mixture of loathing and fear, and went to work. And he worked with concentration. He even began to warm up to Dunlap's assistant (who rode a motorcycle), but Dunlap himself could not get through to him.

The barriers did not come down until the day before the show was scheduled to move uptown to NBC. Dunlap had invited his father, who was in New York on a visit from Iowa, to lunch at McSorley's Ale House, a few steps from the rehearsal hall. When they came out of the old saloon, Dunlap spotted Jimmy in the street signaling a cab, and asked if he would mind sharing the ride uptown. Jimmy said no. During the ride Jimmy found out that Dunlap's father was "an old farmer from Ioway" and the two got into an animated discussion of hogs: Poland Chinas, Tamworths, Hampshires. Jimmy was delighted to discover that Dunlap was a farm kid like himself. In the remaining rehearsals he gave the director complete cooperation.

Later that same month, Jimmy got another important role, appearing with Dorothy Gish, Vaughn Taylor, and Ed Begley in a "Robert Montgomery Presents" drama, *Harvest*. On the CBS series, "Danger," he co-starred with Mildred Dunnock in *Padlocks*. At rehearsals, she remembers, "He might be two minutes late, never terribly late, and he would come in like something shot out of a cannon and literally walk up the walls. I mean, you know how you can walk up the walls: you've got enough momentum—you just walk up the wall. And people were afraid of him. I mean, not afraid of him, but tentative with him, because he was so physically expressive. He was always extremely gentle with me.

"You don't meet many exciting people in your life. You meet a lot of people you like, a lot of people who are damned good, but you don't see much fire. And when you meet fire, well—my life is the extension of life through my acting. And that holds more for me, my imagination holds more for me than any reality I've ever known. And I think perhaps this was true for Jimmy—no reality ever came up to his imagination. And so he was always disappointed."

In a "Philco Playhouse" drama, *Run Like a Thief*, Jimmy played a resort hotel bellboy who is suspected by owners Kurt Kasznar and Gusti Huber of plotting to steal jewelry. "He was a little bit strange," Kasznar recalls, "but he impressed me a great deal. He was a tremendously good actor. We're rehearsing a scene and Jimmy is difficult. He keeps on saying, 'I don't understand the motive. I can't do it that way. Give me a reason. Why do I have to do it this way?' 'Well,' says the director, 'there's going to be a red light and that's the camera shooting; it might not be on you, it might move and so forth'—but Jimmy never admitted to understanding this medium. I felt so bad—it was the fourth day or so of rehearsal—that Gusti and I went in to see the director and said, 'Unless he stops this nonsense, which is holding us up, you know—we're not playing any scenes. He's playing theatre. I know I have to stand that far behind Gusti in order to make the scene possible.' Jimmy would not stand where he was told. And it became a thing. There was a discussion. And then once he went to lunch with the director and came back very apologetic. And then there was a coffee break and he went downstairs after asking to be excused for fifteen minutes and from one of those lobby stores he brought me a Brahms Requiem and Gusti some kind of a Catholic medal. He wanted to say, 'I didn't mean to hurt anybody.' And everything was much better for the next few days.

"There is a scene which plays in our bedroom and the jewelry is under the mattress. And I dismiss him and he leaves. The next scene I am alone with Gusti and that is the key point of the play. Jimmy storms out and he doesn't close the door. Now the requisite is that the door be closed. So the director says to Jimmy, 'Close the door.' And Jimmy says: 'I just can't close the door. The way I'm walking I cannot close the door. It's impossible.' 'Don't you understand?' I say to him. 'If you stand at the door and overhear us the whole plot is out the window.' And he said, 'I can't.' But finally, the day before we went into the studio, he closes the door. And then we go to the studio for dress rehearsal and he leaves the door open! And then comes the show and he leaves the door open! And I'm not saying anything against him, but there was something that bugged him, something that he felt —that he was, at that time, so far above live television crap, or whatever it can be called. He felt that he was going to be a star. He was convinced that he was going to be a star. He was convinced that he was right. And as for behaving the way he did, I felt that he couldn't help it somehow, that he didn't know the difference between being nice and being ornery."

Word soon got around that James Dean was "difficult to work with." Television directors of that era were as much prisoners of the network system as Hollywood directors were of the studio system. Product was king, not art. Directors got high marks for quantity, not quality. In this assembly-line atmosphere, Jimmy's habit of interrupting rehearsals to ask probing questions about his character's motivation, about the author's intent, or even about the director's interpretation, didn't win him any popularity contests. Jane Deacy trusted Jimmy's sincerity and encouraged him to go for his own truth; but other people in the business were suspicious: Jimmy Dean was only playing ego games, being obnoxious, silly, even stupid!

Television directors preferred working with "seasoned professionals," actors who would appear on time, learn their lines, stand where they were told, and who, above all, would not attack the script. They were indeed seasoned or, as Elia Kazan put it, in an interview with *Cahiers du Cinéma:* "The more success an actor has, the more he acquires the look of wax fruit: he is no longer devoured by life. I try to catch my actors at the moment when they are still, or again human. And if you have a human actor, at that moment, you can slip your hand inside, touch him and wake him . . . Jimmy Dean was just a young fellow who prowled about the front offices. But he had violence in him, he had hunger."

It's not surprising that most directors weren't eager to find themselves in the same studio with Jimmy. Wax fruit was perfect. It would never show bruises or rotten spots in the all-but-still-life dramas they were arranging in front of the cameras. Even those directors who did have the intelligence and intuition to recognize Jimmy's talent found it difficult to face him on the set. He reminded them only too painfully of the early phases of their own careers when they, too, had burned with dreams and dedication.

Most of the roles Jimmy played on television were similar. He would be cast as an emotionally deprived adolescent fighting for affection and understanding in a cold, chaotic world. Usually, too, the character's need for love would be hopelessly frustrated and he would fling himself into a cruel confrontation with authority: father, mother, teachers, bosses, cops.

His first stage role, Wally Wilkins in *See the Jaguar*, had been an almost clinically exaggerated version of this stereotype. His second stage role, Bachir in *The Immoralist*, would again make him an adolescent victim, but this time with power to seduce and destroy.

Gide's novel told the story of a man who marries, only to discover, on his honeymoon, that he is a homosexual. Ruth Goetz, who, with her husband Augustus, would eventually turn *The Immoralist* into a play, had been fascinated by the story ever since she had first read it while working for the book's American publisher, Alfred Knopf.

After Ruth and Augustus triumphed in London with

The Heiress, a play based on Henry James's *Washington Square,* they decided to fly over to Paris and approach Gide with the idea of adapting *The Immoralist* for the stage.

Although he received the two writers with great courtesy, Gide was firm in his refusal to grant them permission to base a play on his book. He said simply that he couldn't imagine how it could be done. The story wasn't dramatic material. But Ruth Goetz was determined. She continued, in her excellent French, to argue the case.

"There is a quality one must have in the theatre," she said boldly.

"Oh," said Gide, as cool as ever. "And what is that, Madame?"

"La fatalité," said Ruth, gambling everything on one roll of the tongue.

Gide opened his eyes a bit. For the first time in the conversation, he nodded.

"Yes," he said, after a painfully slow moment, "that's what that book is about."

He gave his consent to the project.

When the adaptation was finished, Billy Rose optioned it and hired Herman Shumlin to direct. After Geraldine Page and Louis Jourdan had agreed to do the honeymoon couple, Shumlin called James Dean in to read for the boy, Bachir. "Herman opened the door of Billy's study," says Ruth Goetz, "and a young creature entered, who was, of course, really twenty years before his time. I had never seen anyone dressed that way in my life. Jimmy did role-playing in his dress before I even knew of it. He had borrowed some finery for this audition. He had on a Russian fur hat. He had on his blue jeans, of which he had only one pair and in which there was a large hole, not for role-playing, that was just the necessities of life. He had on a pair of borrowed boots, like rodeo boots. They were either too big for him or too small, I don't know which, but I knew that they hurt. He had on a vest and coat that had to be sixty years old. It was old formal wear.

"He said he would like to read the scene in which Bachir is supposed to be cleaning. Herman said all right, he would read the woman's part. It was a brief scene on the terrace—he's a lazy little louse and he hasn't done any of the housework. And Jimmy got down onto the floor and he was into the part and he was dazzling!

"He read no more than three or four minutes. I forgot his appearance, his looks, his un-beauty, his starvedness, his, I would have said, Scotch-Irish antecedents. I don't know what they were, but he was fatally blond—blondish, reddish-blond, with pale skin. I thought, none of that matters, he's so talented. This is it.

"Now after that glorious introduction, where it was obvious to all of us that he was great, we go into rehearsal and the little son-of-a-bitch was one of the most unspeakably detestable fellows to work with I ever knew in my life. The little bastard would not learn the words, would not really try to give a performance, would not really rehearse. He was absolutely contemptuous of Herman, who was responsible for getting him the job. Herman would say something to him and he would make a point of not doing it. He drove us up the wall. Gus and me he ignored. The only person that he made a connection to was Geraldine Page, because Gerry was an artist, an artist whom he could understand. And she had great fellow feeling for him."

Jimmy got the Bachir part at the end of November 1953. Rehearsals at Billy Rose's Ziegfeld Theatre, which stood at Fifty-fourth and Sixth Avenue until it was sky-scrapered out of existence, went on through the Christmas season. Day by day Ruth and Augustus grew more and more worried about Jimmy's performance (or lack of it). They began to discuss the possibility of replacing him. Geraldine Page advised against it. So did Herman Shumlin. Both said Jimmy would turn in a great Bachir. Billy Rose had no opinion on the subject, because, unlike most producers, he was staying away from rehearsals as a mark of his complete confidence in Herman, Ruth, and Augustus.

Jimmy's role was not big, but it was the fulcrum on which the whole dramatic seesaw of *The Immoralist* balanced. Bachir played brilliantly would produce the feeling of fatality that Ruth had made such a point of to Gide. Bachir played badly would turn fatality to farce, or worse, to camp.

And Jimmy's lack of enthusiasm wasn't the only problem that concerned Ruth and Gus. They were beginning to have doubts about the director, too. They didn't like the way Shumlin was handling the all-important scene in which Bachir tries to seduce the husband. It was essential that its homosexual content be absolutely clear. The boy knew what he was up to, and the audience had to know that he knew. Shumlin wasn't directing for that result. He didn't even seem to understand that it was important.

Finally Ruth and Gus asked Billy Rose to come to a rehearsal. He came, he saw, he agreed with them. The new director was Daniel Mann.

But Jimmy was not replaced, and early in January the embattled troupe set off to the City of Brotherly Love, where at the Forrest Theatre, the play was to try out.

"We got to Philadelphia," says Ruth, "and began putting it all together. It was a nightmare. Jimmy was awful, and we had all kinds of technical difficulty and a lot of rewriting to do.

"But we started up and Jimmy gave us a very good opening night's performance and then was absolutely ghastly for the next two, three, or four days, to the point where Billy was ready to do him in. He got hold of Jimmy during a rehearsal and he said, 'You young punk, if you don't do your work, I'm going to smash you!' There was an ugly, angry fight and, of course, that night Jimmy was better.

"Gerry's performance was fine always. She was a rock. Jourdan got very much better and did very well for us. They all got steadily better except this little monster who was great one night and appalling the next.

"While we were in Philadelphia, there was an awful lot of comment about the play in the New York press. Bob Anderson had *Tea and Sympathy* coming in at the same time, which Gadge (Elia Kazan) was producing, and Gadge was very eager to see what we had. And I didn't even know that he came down to Philadelphia, but he did come down; and he saw Jimmy Dean, and he caught him in a matinee, and he caught him good. He must have seen one of the few good performances that Jimmy gave us in Philadelphia. We knew nothing of this, of course.

"But, in any case, Jimmy was pissed off with us, obviously because we had been so rough on him, and opening night in New York, he gave us a fine performance, a really great performance, but when it was over, at eleven o'clock, he gave his notice!

"And when we heard about it, we were stunned—the opening night in New York for a young actor who's just made a hit. What . . . what does he mean?' And he had told the stage manager he was leaving, so Danny Mann, our director, went back to talk to him to find out what the hell was up, and Jimmy said: 'I've got an offer. I can do a movie for Gadge Kazan. He's doing a movie called *East of Eden.*' And Gadge did that, and I thought it was a stinking trick.

"Well, after Jimmy knew that he had done that to us, he gave us three weeks of unparalleled brilliance so that nobody who followed him could possibly be as good."

Jimmy enjoyed himself in those weeks. It was good to be earning money, and he used some of it to buy himself a motorcycle, the first he'd had since Fairmount. One night he brought it backstage, right into Geraldine Page's dressing room, and tried to talk her into taking a ride with him.

By this time she knew Jimmy and liked him and was hardly ever surprised at anything he did, but when she had first met him, during an early rehearsal of *The Immoralist*, he had really amazed her.

She looked around her and saw that all the actors were on their best behavior, ever so eager to please the director. Then she realized that she hadn't noticed one young man, slumped down, cap pulled over his glasses, collar turned up. That, she guessed, must be Jimmy Dean.

During the very first scene Shumlin began giving the actors line readings (indicating to them the exact rhythm and tone of their speeches). They were horrified by this scorn for their artistic integrity, but nobody dared say anything. It came time for Jimmy to read. He mumbled his first line almost inaudibly.

"I beg your pardon," said Shumlin. "The first line, you should read it this way. Ta-dum, ta-DUM, ta-dum."

There was a silence. Finally Jimmy said: "Mr. Shumlin, why are you insulting my intelligence?"

The other actors waited for an explosion. It didn't come.

"I didn't mean to do that," Shumlin said quietly. "How did I insult your intelligence?"

"Well," said Jimmy, "it's the first reading and you want me to read the line a certain way. I would like to have time to get used to who the people are that I'm supposed to be talking to and have a chance to decide some things first."

Now the storm would certainly break.

But Shumlin only said, "I'm very sorry."

Geraldine Page knew that she was going to like this new young actor.

The Immoralist opened on February 8, 1954, Jimmy's twenty-third birthday. The reviews were not raves, but they were respectful. In the *Herald Tribune*, Walter Kerr said: "In adapting André Gide's *The Immoralist* for the stage, Ruth and Augustus Goetz have brought a quiet patient candor to the subject of homosexuality, but a quiet patient candor is not precisely an exhilarating theatrical vein. There is taste in abundance in the writing and the directing and the acting at the Royale, but there is very little emotion. . . . James Dean makes a colorfully insinuating scapegrace."

In the *Post* Richard Watts said: "James Dean is realistically unpleasant as the slimy one." In the *World-Telegram* William Hawkins said: "It is James Dean as the house-boy who clearly and originally underlines the sleazy impertinence and the immoral opportunism which the husband must combat."

Once again, Jimmy had done better than the play. His work as Bachir earned him a Daniel Blum Theatre World Award as "the best newcomer of the year."

EIGHT

A few days after Jimmy left the cast of *The Immoralist*,
Warner Brothers released the news of his big break. The
March 6, 1954 New York *Times* theatrical pages carried
the following item: "James Dean, who originated the
role of the young Arab servant in the Broadway offering,
The Immoralist, has been signed by Elia Kazan for the
male lead in the forthcoming Warner Bros. version of
John Steinbeck's novel *East of Eden*."

The hero Jimmy Dean was about to embody had been
evolving through many decades. In the beginning, the
good guy wore a white hat, defended the sacred ethic of
private property to the death, but seldom died, and always, if he lived, got the girl. In doing so, he defeated
the bad guys (in black hats), prevented the white virgin
from being raped (at least by the bad guys), and bru-
tally murdered lots of dark-skinned people, mostly Indi-
ans and Mexicans.

Then, somehow, in the depression-paralyzed thirties,
the bad guys began to seem more likable. It wasn't so

easy to support the old "hang 'em for stealing a loaf of bread" morality when people were actually going hungry. Heroes like Cagney got shot down on church steps. Others, like Garfield, staggered across the threshold of Home Sweet Home to die in Mom's arms. The camera was doing less looking down from on high, more looking up from down under. It was hard to hate anybody you really got to know.

In the forties, Bogart's hard-nosed, soft-hearted hero moved the image even further toward the middle of the good-and-evil scale. He knew that he was condemned to be corrupt by a corrupt society. He knew he had to cheat and kill to survive. But that didn't prevent him from doing as much good as he could along the way.

So maybe there really were two sides to every story, and maybe, at least at times, the bad side was actually the good one. On closer inspection, there seemed to be some holes in the holy fabric of private property and racism.

Then, in 1947, Marlon Brando "Hey Stellaed" his way into the national consciousness in Tennessee Williams' *A Streetcar Named Desire* (with Kazan as conductor). Here was the hero, profoundly vulnerable, so deeply sensitive that he had to pretend not to care at all just to survive. The bad and the brutal had become the saintly. Kowalski was a mumbling, illiterate martyr to the prejudices of an etiolated ruling class. Who could blame him for snatching a few moments of sensual conquest as an escape from his awareness of the oblivion for which society had destined him?

But, by 1954, Brando, the "young rebel," was no longer quite so young. He was, at least in the studio's opinion, ready for the more stable Hollywood orbit of versatile but dependable star. Kazan needed a new body to fit the boots and jacket.

Warner Brothers' synopsis of the film will give some idea of the hero Kazan was trying to find.

EAST OF EDEN

Among the students rushing from classes at the end of the day, Aron Trask (RICHARD DAVALOS) and his girl friend, Abra (JULIE HARRIS), are joined by Aron's brother, Cal (JAMES DEAN). He follows the couple to an ice house where their father, Adam Trask (RAYMOND MASSEY), is excitedly explaining to Will Hamilton (ALBERT DEKKER) his plan to keep vegetables fresh by refrigeration. In introducing his two sons, Adam plainly reveals that Aron is his favorite. That evening, Cal learns from Sheriff Sam Cooper (BURL IVES) his mother, who deserted Adam years before, is Kate (JO VAN FLEET), owner of a notorious gambling and dance hall. When Adam's refrigeration project fails, Cal, anxious to win his father's affection, enters into a profitable venture with Will. One night at an amusement park, Cal offers Abra a ride on the ferris wheel. She protests her love for Aron but passionately returns Cal's kiss. At Adam's birthday celebration, Cal makes elaborate preparations to present to his father all the profits from the speculation.

However, Adam reprimands his son for profiteering and Cal is further denounced by his brother. With that, Cal decides to reveal the secret of their mother. Following the meeting with his mother and discovering Abra's love for Cal, it is a drunken and completely changed Aron who bids Adam farewell before departing to join the Army. Stricken by the turn of events, Adam is carried home. There, as Abra pleads, Adam finally acknowledges Cal, blesses them both.

With the exception of the euphemism "dance hall" for whore house, this is the story that screenwriter Paul Osborn rendered from Steinbeck's fat novel.

"When I introduced John to Dean," says Kazan, "I mean, when I introduced Dean to John, I took Dean up there and John liked him right away for the part. He said, 'Jesus Christ, he is Cal'; which is pretty close to the truth —he was.

"As an actor, Jimmy was tremendously sensitive, what they used to call an instrument. You could see through his feelings. He was so twisted and sick. People said he was like Brando. Nothing like Brando at all. He had very little pliability. He had sort of one hurt, a very hurt person. The main thing you felt about him is hurt. And the main thing the girls felt, and the boys felt about him, the faggots felt about him, was that you'd want to put your arm around him and protect him and look after him— don't worry kid, I'm on your side.

"He was suffused with self-pity, even though he never expressed a lot of it, but he was just suffused with the anguish of rejection. And the other actors were all very concerned about him. He was the luckiest guy in the world he got Julie Harris to work with, because he could have gotten a girl that just got angry at him and castrated him. He was easily castrated. He could have gotten a girl that just froze him. But she is such a kind, decent, lovely, understanding person. She's very much like her character (Abra). She's just a saint, Julie is. She was marvelous with him, took care of him, encouraged him, and supported him. And the other actors all felt he was very talented, which was clear, but above all they felt: you can't beat it, that's the part! It was one of those miracles of casting where it worked out right."

Kazan's memory of how he found Dean differs considerably from Ruth Goetz's account of the discovery. "I never had anybody in mind," he says. "I started to look around. Paul Osborn told me he'd seen a play at the Royale Theatre by Gide, *The Immoralist*, and that Dean did a little bit in there. 'You ought to see him,' he told me. So I called Dean in—I never went to see the play—anyway, I called old Dean in and I just went out and there he was sitting on the bench. And what I try to do is I try to get to talk to people.

"I got talking to him, trying to see what he was really like, and after a while he took me for a ride on the back of his motorbike. That was okay. I'm not keen on motorbikes, but anyway, I had just two or three more meetings with him, but it was obvious right from the beginning that he was really perfect for it. There was never any question. It was only a matter of convincing Warner's that I wanted to do the picture without a star.

"In those days, I'd made a lot of money for them and so they were very keen on letting me do anything I wanted. And also, they were better off. So then I did say I want to do it with this kid. That's all there was to it. They said okay.

"I don't think (Jack) Warner even saw him. And then, when I brought him out to California, he didn't even have any luggage, for Christ's sake. He just had some paper packages and bags. Looked like he'd never been up in a plane before. He kept looking out the window of the plane to see why the fuck it was going in the air and how it was held up there. Well not quite that naïve. I had a limousine pick me up and pick him up with his paper packages. But, anyway, we got out there and, I don't know where it was, somebody found him a home, some agent or somebody, Dick Clayton."

The "home" Dick Clayton, Jimmy's Hollywood agent, found for him was a double room over a drugstore opposite Warner Brothers' Burbank lot. During the early weeks of shooting, Jimmy shared these quarters with Dick Davalos, a gifted young actor who was playing his brother, Aron. It wasn't long before Jimmy began subjecting Davalos to the same sort of hot-and-cold, on-and-off moods he had inflicted on Bill Bast. Davalos finally decided that he had had it, told Jimmy so plainly, and thenceforth ignored him except when he was forced to speak to him in character on the set. Off the set, Jimmy began to tag after Davalos, whining and apologizing. But Davalos refused to be a sucker a second time.

Kazan's instinct told him that he'd better keep closer watch on his young lead. "I was living off in some apartment. My wife and children weren't with me. I got the idea of moving into a dressing room on the lot. And I got the next dressing room for him. So he was under my thumb all the time. I could watch him, encourage him, and see to it that he wasn't bedeviled by anything. They were large dressing rooms: they had a sitting room and a bedroom and a bathroom and kitchen—star quarters. And there were two empty there, door to door. So I moved into one and I moved him into the other and it was very nice. It relieved me, and also allowed him to get a lot of sleep. He didn't have to drive so much. I was afraid of his driving—ever since he took me rumbling around on the motorbike. Jesus, I never would have gone if I'd known about his fucking bad eyes. But in California, I finally had to say to him: 'No more motorbike until you get through with the picture. Go out and kill yourself after you're done, but don't drive any more.' I had to impress that on him. So he gave it up for the time being. And it was very nice on the lot and he was very, very good. He worked hard because he knew it would change his life."

Jimmy did work hard. He thought out every scene in advance, and often did bits of business in front of the camera that he had not previously discussed with either Kazan or the other actors. In the birthday party sequence Cal makes his father a present of the money he has earned by speculating on a wartime bean crop. His father refuses to accept what he considers tainted profits. Instead of running out the door right away, Jimmy pushed the bills into Raymond Massey's face and then flung himself at him, sobbing and whimpering. Massey's reaction, which was real shock, worked perfectly for the father's surprise and confusion. Kazan kept the take.

"Massey," says Kazan, "didn't like Jimmy because Jimmy was the opposite of all Massey's training and technique. And Jimmy surprised me, too. He did some wonderful things. He threw his arms around Massey in that self-pitying, pathetic gesture. He just pulled that on Massey and I thought it was marvelous, terrific. He was very quick. He'd do everything in a very personal and distinctive way. The business in that scene on top of the railroad car was his idea, too. He put his arms inside the sweater and then he took the sleeves of the sweater and wrapped them around his neck. He looked like a little frozen monkey up there. That's him. All alone in the world, misunderstood, out in the cold."

In the winter of 1954, Julie Harris starred in a Broadway production of Jean Anouilh's *Mademoiselle Colombe*. In the spring, Kazan asked her to do a color test with Jimmy Dean. "I made a test," she remembers, "with Gjon Mili (a photographer who frequently contributed to the now defunct *Life* magazine). He took a color test of Jimmy and me. The first time I remember meeting Jim— I didn't see *The Immoralist*, I missed him in that. Guess I'd never seen him on stage—first time I met him was at some party down in the Village—the opening night of some play, at the Theatre de Lys, I think. Jimmy was there and we were introduced and he looked at me, kind of quizzically and he said, 'Well, how did you like playing in *The Moon Is Blue?*' (which had, in fact, starred Barbara Bel Geddes). And I thought, what's he doing, is he putting me on? And I said, 'I wasn't in *The Moon Is Blue.*' I never was in it. And he kind of looked at me and smiled. And I was very square and said, 'I really wasn't in that *Moon Is Blue.*' He didn't say very much after that.

Julie Harris next encountered Jimmy at photographer Gjon Mili's studio on Fourteenth Street. Kazan had called and asked her to let Mili take some color shots of her and Jimmy. But it didn't turn out to be a regular screen test— they didn't work on a scene, they improvised—and so she suspected that Kazan was only really interested in seeing if the difference in ages (she was a few years older than Jimmy) would show up on film.

Jimmy roared up on his motorcycle, stashed it between two cars, came clopping up the studio stairs sloppy and unshaven. Mili said simply, "You'll have to shave!" showed Jimmy to a sink, and gave him a razor. While photographer and actress waited and watched, Jimmy transformed a simple shave into an elaborate ritual, all the while throwing out ideas for the pictures. He'd brought along some balloons. He and Julie could pretend they were at the carnival in the *East of Eden* script.

Then, putting down the razor, and puffing out his freshly shaved cheeks, he blew up the balloons, and soon he and Julie were dancing about and Mili was snapping pictures. "Jimmy was fascinating," Julie Harris remembers. "He was like a chameleon. You weren't quite sure

what he was doing. At one point I was putting my hands
up to my face. And he said, 'Why do you do that?' And I
thought, what is he doing? He's telling me how to act. Or
he's giving me lessons. I said, 'I don't know why I do
that.' And he said, 'Well, maybe it's because you want to
seem as if you're younger than you are. Because you're
older than I am and that makes you seem younger.' And
I said, 'Well, I don't do it for that reason, I just do it.
Maybe it's a characteristic, maybe it's a habit pattern.'
So, anyway, I felt like he was putting me on, trying to put
me in my place. So in my mind I said, I don't care. So I
didn't fight him. I just let him say whatever he wanted to
say because I felt that he was kind of on the defensive and
I wanted him to like me."

The very night Julie Harris got to Hollywood, there
was a knock on her door. It was Jimmy. "Come on out,"
he said. "I want to show you something." He took her
out to the street and showed her a little red MG. He had
just bought it. He asked her to come for a drive.

"So," she remembers, "he took me for this wild ride up
into the Hollywood hills. I was holding on. I thought I
was going to fall out. It really felt just like I had to hold
onto the seat to stay in the car. I wasn't going to say,
'Slow down, Jimmy!' I knew that would just make him go
all the faster. He was testing me to see if I'd take everything he had to give. Then we stopped somewhere and
we looked out at the hills. When he drove me home, I
thanked him, and he left. From then on he never did anything like that. We were very close. We had a wonderful
time working together and he never told me what to do.

"Jimmy was like a Tom Sawyer to me. Like he would get everybody to paint the fence and be standing there saying: What a great job you're all doing! He did manipulate people. And knew he was doing it. Because he was very brilliant and there was nothing he couldn't do as far as acting went. He knew exactly when and what. He was terribly sensitive with me. I felt we really were doing the parts. That when he looked at me, in the scene, I was Abra to him. I was his brother's girl. And I was always saying, trying to say in my mind: Don't look at me as Aron's girl, look at me as just Abra.

"When we were working on the ice house scene, Jimmy was always around. In that scene there was always that presence. I mean, he kept the story going, he was really so much in it. He was different with everybody: when he watched his mother (Jo Van Fleet), when he spoke to Will, the part that Albert Dekker played, and with his father—yes, I think inside he probably really loved Ray Massey. Really loved him. But he was working with that feeling that this was a man who was not his generation, who didn't want him to say—well, Jimmy would always say a lot of, would swear. I can't remember now. I remember some of what he'd say—'Fuck,' or something like that, and Ray would turn scarlet and finally had to say, once: 'You mustn't talk like that; there are ladies present.' Which just egged Jimmy on more.

"But it was a matter of people really creeping into these parts. It's so hard in movie work to make the story really come alive, day by day. I think all of us were really doing it. We were really carrying it over in our minds.

145

"I was never in the habit of falling in love with younger men. But if I had had the misfortune to really fall in love with Jimmy, I would have been in trouble. But I didn't. I wasn't involved with him that way. And he, in fact, toward the beginning of shooting, fell in love with Pier Angeli, who was making a picture (*The Silver Chalice*) on the same lot. And they were introduced and he used to say to me: how could it be that this love had come to him just at the right time in his life? It had made him so sensitive to everything, caring about her. And she had given him a little enameled locket, like an Egyptian mummy. It was very beautiful and it opened up, and inside, he showed me, was a little piece of material from the dress that she wore when they first met and a lock of her hair. He wore that around his neck. And he was so happy with her.

"I'm sure the family was frightened for Pier. I remember once she had asked some friends to have lunch in the commissary and I guess she'd said to Jimmy, would he come to lunch? And he came without a shirt, dirty from the set, in his old dungarees. And Pier—she was, in those days, a beautifully perfect little creature. I mean, she was always in an ensemble, always completely perfect, bag, shoes, everything, and just a little hat or bandanna. And every day was a different outfit. She burst into tears when he appeared at lunch this way, and so they weren't talking for a time.

"And later on he bought a camera, or Gadge bought him a camera, or told him what to get, like a Rolleiflex, and he started to take pictures around the set. And he

Wreckage of the Porsche Spyder in which Jimmy died in the late afternoon of
September 30, 1955, on Route 466 (now 46), near Cholame, California.

James Dean's grave in Park Cemetery, Fairmount, Indiana. Over the years souvenir hunters have chiselled countless chips off the stone. Note the badly defaced inscription.

talked to me about his plans. He hoped to make movies. He was fascinated with the lights and why they were doing that this way, and this that way. He wanted to do Exupéry's *Le Petit Prince*, that's the picture he wanted to make. And then I saw that Lenny Rosenman was teaching him how to read music and he was playing Bach on his recorder. You'd stumble upon him playing Bach and he looked like an angel. He really was a beautiful boy. Beautiful. And he had a great talent for drawing too. He was fascinated with everything.

"And I remember the last day. It was terrible for me. You always feel that you're alone in these feelings, whatever you feel, you feel nobody else can possibly be experiencing that. The last I was shot—I don't know what scene we worked on. It was the exterior of the house, I know that. And there was to be a party that night, I guess, given somewhere. It was awful for me that last day to think it had all gone away, that life that we'd been leading for two and a half months. You wouldn't see anybody again. You wouldn't come there every day. You wouldn't look forward to it. It was just gone. And I remember looking around and thinking, I've got to say good-bye to Jimmy. And suddenly, all the set was just deserted and everybody had gone. And he had a dressing room, portable dressing room caravan, on the set, and I went up to the caravan and knocked on the door and I thought I heard something like a sob. I said, 'Jimmy,' and then I knocked again. So then I was sure it was a sob and I opened the door and he was just in tears, his eyes—and

I said, 'What's the matter?' and he said, 'It's over, it's over'; and he was like a little boy, so lonely."

But not every woman responded to Jimmy as sympathetically as Julie Harris. After Warner's PR chief invited Hedda Hopper to lunch in the studio commissary to meet James Dean, the new young "genius," she reported: "In my business, I get 'genius' dished out to me as regularly as the morning mail. To believe the press agents, every dirty-shirttail boy in blue jeans who comes over the hill from Lee Strasberg's Actors Studio is the biggest thing to hit the industry since Jack Barrymore played Don Juan. Ninety-nine times out of a hundred the gangling lad is like a dream brought on by eating Port Salut cheese too late at night. If you wait long enough, it goes away."

The meeting turned out to be a non-meeting. Jimmy slouched in from the set as dirty or dirtier than he had been on the day he so shocked Pier Angeli. There he flopped down at a table near Miss Hopper's, put his feet up on a chair and eyed her with all the warmth of a wild animal just brought into captivity. A moment later he jumped up, scanned the line of framed stars on the wall, fixed on one, spat in his eyes, wiped the glass clean with a handkerchief, slammed back down into his chair and began wolfing his food.

Miss Hopper firmly declined the embarrassed PR chief's offer to bring Jimmy to her table. She had already made up her mind what she was going to tell her typewriter when she got back to the office.

So, for a few more months, until sneak previews of

East of Eden began to generate the sort of excitement that announces a new star, Jimmy's private life, which in that period was his affair with Pier Angeli, remained his business and hers.

Anna (that was her real first name) Pierangeli was the only woman, other than his mother (who was also small and dark-haired), Jimmy ever loved. Anna and Marisa (later Marisa Pavan) Pierangeli were non-identical twins. They were born on June 19, 1933, on the island of Sardinia. While they were still children, their father, architect Luigi Pierangeli, moved the family to Rome where he became an important designer and builder. They were six years old when World War II broke out.

Pier remembered that her father had to bicycle out into the countryside to find peasants who might be willing to sell him a little milk, a few vegetables. Then the Nazis occupied the city. The Pierangelis' life grew even more difficult. Finally, in 1945, the war ended.

Having survived the Fascisti, the Nazis, and near starvation, the family began bit by bit to regain its sense of security, only to suffer a different, perhaps even more painful trauma when, as a school girl of fifteen, Pier was raped by an American soldier.

A year later, Vittorio De Sica offered Pier a small part in his film, *Tomorrow Is Too Late.* Her father refused flatly. But Pier's mother, who had given up her own stage career to marry, pleaded with him until he gave his permission.

Pier was already hauntingly beautiful. "As soon as I saw the child," De Sica said, "her fragile body, her sensitive face, I knew she was the right one." One of the scenes called for a young actor to kiss Pier. When he did, she fainted.

Shortly after the De Sica picture was finished, Stewart Stern, who would later write the script for *Rebel Without a Cause*, put Pier in her first American film, *Teresa*. A few weeks after finishing *Teresa*, Pier signed the studio contract which would take her to Hollywood. Her father, worn out by the war, died of a heart attack.

When the fatherless family got to Hollywood, Signora Pierangeli wouldn't let Pier out of her sight. Wherever Pier went, Mama went—to the studio, to openings, to parties, even on dates. The Signora was always present, watching, warning, scolding, advising.

Pier was twenty-one the summer she met Jimmy. It had been a tremendously important birthday. For the first time she was allowed her own checking account (her first check went for a sapphire ring), a car (a baby-blue Cadillac convertible), and permission to go out on dates without Mama.

"Jeemy," she said, "is a wonderful boy, a great actor. But we are very young. He will soon be twenty-four. This is the first year for me I am allowed to go out alone. There is a very old joke in Hollywood. If a boy dates me, they say he must also date my mother, my two sisters (Marisa and the younger Patrizia), my dogs and my parakeets. This is not true anymore."

Even though Signora Pierangeli allowed Pier to see Jimmy, she made it clear that she disapproved. Agent Dick Clayton remembers one of her more aggressive ploys. "Jimmy wanted to get in touch with Pier, but her mother changed the phone number and he couldn't get to talk to her. So I got the number for him. He was shooting at Warner's and I was out there walking along with my boss Charlie Feldman and we ran into Jack Warner and we stopped and we were talking over a few things. So along came Jimmy and he hopped right over and said hello to everybody and I slipped him a piece of paper and said, 'Here's the number you want.' So he screamed and howled and he grabbed me and gave me a kiss and a hug and he was just like a kid. It was like giving him a great prize."

Jimmy was serious about Pier. To take her out he would even get into a tuxedo. "Pier Angeli is a raro person," he said in a fan magazine interview. "Unlike most Hollywood girls, she is real and genuine. Her only trouble is that she gets confused by listening to too many advisors."

On one of their very first dates, Jimmy took Pier to dinner at Frascati's with his father and his stepmother. Pier liked the Deans. "They are wonderful people," she said afterward.

On Sunday, their only day off from shooting, Jimmy often took Pier out to the Pacific Palisades home of Gene Owen, the woman who had taught him acting at Santa Monica College. Mrs. Owen had not heard from Jimmy since he left for New York, but when he came back to work in *East of Eden,* he had taken time to drive down to Santa Monica and surprise her.

She was teaching when he arrived. Rather than disturb

ner, he waited in the corridor. As she stepped out of the classroom, he scooped her into his arms and carried her all the way down the hall to her office. She was even more amazed when he told her he was starring in an Elia Kazan movie. She couldn't get over it. Only five years earlier, he had been just another terrified freshman.

Mrs. Owen remembers one Sunday visit in particular. Pier and Jimmy arrived in his little red MG and spent the entire afternoon trying to recover from the shock of a near-collision on Sunset Boulevard. Over and over, Jimmy promised Pier that he would drive more carefully in the future.

When Jimmy wasn't seeing Pier, he would spend his evenings at Arthur Loew Jr.'s house on Miller Drive, not far from the apartment he had rented at 1741 Sunset Plaza Drive. Arthur Loew Jr., whose grandfather Marcus Loew founded Metro-Goldwyn-Mayer, and whose grandfather Adolph Zucker founded Paramount, was an important but little publicized personage in the Hollywood of that era. By day, he worked as a producer at Metro; by night, he played host to a galaxy of Hollywood personalities. His friendships range all the way from Louis Calhern to Paul Newman, from Elizabeth Taylor to Eartha Kitt.

"The first time I ran into Jimmy," he says, "I was going with Pier Angeli, the Italian actress that Stewart Stern discovered. I used to see her—and then, years later, I started seeing her sister, Marisa, and it was during that time that I went to pick Marisa up one day and I walked into the house (in Brentwood) and I saw Anna (Pier), her sister, out in the yard with this guy. I started to open the door to say hello to her and Marisa said, 'Hey, don't disturb them.' And I said, 'Disturb whom?' And she said, 'Jimmy's here and he's rehearsing.' And I said, 'Who's Jimmy?' And she said, 'James Dean.' And I said, 'Who's James Dean?' And she said, 'The fabulous New York actor.' 'Never heard of him,' I said. I thought it was a bunch of shit. Some young guy I'd never heard of is rehearsing in the yard and everybody is walking around the house on tiptoe like Laurence Olivier is out there.

"Anyway, a couple of months later, Keenan Wynn, who is a friend of mine, and Rod Steiger, whom I just was getting to know, stopped by the house and they had Jimmy in tow.

"Now, as I recall, he was given the same kind of an entrance. I think he was out in the car, and Keenan and Rod came in and said, 'Listen we got Jimmy Dean and, you know, he's'—in effect they were saying the same thing Marisa had said, you know, this guy you've got to handle with kid gloves or he's liable to go into a mood or a rage. Sort of like saying, this girl is a virgin—you can't say darn. So he comes in, and he was kind of down in the mouth, kind of heavy, as he would appear on the screen sometimes. At any rate, Keenan and I had had a long rapport, we'd done a lot of shows together and always had fun, and Rod would appreciate the humor, and so we started drinking and I did start to pick on him, Jimmy. I think I described my first encounter with him—well, it wasn't much of an encounter because of the fact that when I went in I had to take my shoes off so I wouldn't make noise. And I made it a great parody. So he started to laugh. He enjoyed being sort of made fun of, I guess. And he loosened up. And they said—he went to the bathroom or something—Rod said, it was very unusual because usually—and I didn't know whether it was unusual or maybe just nobody had ever bothered to kid around with him. And, not to turn this into a love story, but at this first meeting, I liked him very much and he responded to my kind of humor.

"So from that moment on we saw a lot of each other. He would come to the house almost every day and we would go out and have dinner, or we'd stay home; and he was sort of a fixture, in a sense, during that period. I still knew nothing about him as an actor. The Hollywood concept of an actor was, well, a lot of young people came out and they were given contracts and most of them weren't very talented. They'd do a picture and they'd be forgotten about. So I never really thought much about Jimmy as an actor. We had a good time together.

"So one day he came over and he asked if I'd like to go out to the Valley and see a sneak preview of *East of Eden.* He had never seen it. It was the first showing. So we got Stewart Stern and the three of us drove out there and we had no idea what we were going to see. So anyway, we sit down with this guy, who's just a guy, and we see this movie, and it was really an overwhelming experience. The film was so beautiful, so fantastic. He gave such a performance. It must have been like the first night somebody went to see Barrymore in *Hamlet.* And it was such an awakening, an eye-opener, because here's somebody

you were palling around with for months and you had no
idea of who he was really.

"So we walk out of the picture—first of all, we can't even
talk, we're so—Stewart and I are so overcome by this film
—we get right up and we leave and we get into the car
and finally, I managed to get out the words, 'Let's stop at
the first bar we see,' which was in the Valley, so we did.
We walked in there and we started to have a drink. And
then we say, 'Jesus, Jimmy, you're absolutely fantastic.'
He was very subdued about the whole thing and never
—you know, simply wasn't giddy as a result of it. The point
was that when we went in there, he was just Jimmy Dean
that nobody at Warner Brothers knew except a couple of
people in Publicity. But when the lights went on, he was
a star.

"And they found him, the Warner Brothers people—
they must have stopped everywhere—and slowly, this little bar we were in filled up with Warner Brothers people.
And all of a sudden, he was a king. They were coming up
to the table and saying, Mr. Dean, I'm so and so, and
exactly what they did, and this and that. And so *A Star
Is Born* is really what we witnessed in two and a half
hours or however long the picture was. Because when the
lights went on, everybody was mesmerized and it was
just like—I mean, everybody was stunned. And nothing
happened, you know, the impact of everything just left
everybody like this! So there wasn't any big cheering in
the theatre. But then, as people got their bearings as we
did, they began to—so that night, as I say, he became
a star.

"So, anyway, then I was fully aware of his talent and ability and then we continued to see one another, but it was still on the same basis as before. I mean, a very light—we would go to eat in various places—I mean, he was very casual in those days. Today, everybody's casual, but he was a rebel in the sense that he would have been a hippie or one of those types because he never wanted to get dressed or wear ties. He was always very casual and wasn't interested in going the Chasen's or Mocambo route or any of that. Brando was similar in that respect. Levi's, a leather jacket—so we would go out to places where you didn't have to get all piss elegant. And then, I don't know, he was just around with a lot of the people that I mentioned: Steiger, Newman, Artie Shaw, Walter Pidgeon, Bob Mitchum, Oscar Levant.

"Oscar's daughter was terribly enamored of Jimmy—she was whacked out of her skull about him. They had never met, of course. And Oscar said to me—I think we were at La Scala (a restaurant in Beverly Hills)—that the greatest thrill his daughter could have ever would be to meet Jimmy. So I guess Jimmy—we were together—we went over to Oscar's house and it was kind of late and his daughter was asleep.

"So June, Oscar's wife, said 'C'mon, let's go upstairs.' So we go into the room and the girl is asleep—it's a terrible thing to do to the girl—so June puts Jimmy not far from the bed, and she turns on the light and wakes the girl up and says, 'Jimmy wants to see you.' She got so excited she practically peed in her pants. She was thrilled, she was embarrassed—she was young, you know—but anyway, it was very cute. And the next day, Jimmy told me that she had roped off the part of the room where he was standing and that nobody was to vacuum there. It was like the old Frank Sinatra days. Girls would pick up a cigarette he'd thrown away and put it under glass.

Jimmy loved pranks and practical jokes. He often amused, and sometimes terrified Arthur Loew and the guests at the Miller Drive house. Once he excused himself to go upstairs to the bathroom. Then, in what seemed less than thirty seconds, there was a very loud knock at the front door. Loew opened wide and there stood Jimmy, smiling, pretending that he was just arriving. Later, Loew discovered that the bathroom door was locked from the inside. When he succeeded in forcing it open he examined the bathroom window to see how Jimmy had gotten through it so quickly. The screen was still fastened. Loew still doesn't know how Jimmy managed that trick even though he repeated it several times, without, however, locking the bathroom door on his return engagements. Even Loew's sense of humor had limits.

On another night, those limits were severely tested. Loew and some of his friends decided to take a late ride down Sunset Boulevard. As they drove through the gate headlights came directly at them out of the darkness. There was no way to avoid a head-on collision. Just when Loew thought he had lived his very last moment the headlights split apart and he heard motorcycles roaring by on either side. Jimmy on one motorcycle, a friend on another, had waited outside the gate for hours to pull that stunt.

"The last time I saw Jimmy," says Loew, "he was going to New York and he wanted to borrow an overcoat, so I gave him mine. And he was getting a cold or something and went to sleep, which he did quite often, he'd go to sleep in a chair. And it was quite late and I don't know who else, a couple of other people were there, and everybody'd left. So I woke him up and said, 'It's two o'clock.' So he got up and he had this overcoat that I had given him around his shoulders, and he went to the door and, as I said, he had this cold, so he pitched that overcoat over his shoulder and he said to me, 'The picture business is in very bad shape. I am not feeling well and Barrymore is dead.' Then he just turned and walked out."

In the late fall of 1954, Jimmy and Pier Angeli broke up and Pier married singer Vic Damone, a good Italian kid from Brooklyn. It all happened so quickly that even veteran Hollywood gossipmongers were caught with their rumors down. But they did make it to the church, St. Timothy's, in time to see Jimmy sitting across the street on his motorcycle, torturing himself with the spectacle of the bride and groom's happy honeymoon getaway to Las Vegas.

Months afterward, in New York, Jimmy confessed to Lenny Rosenman that he had beaten Pier up a few nights before the wedding. When asked earlier by *Modern Screen* if he intended to become engaged to Pier, Jimmy had said, "You mean me and Miss Pizza? Who knows? Right now I'm too neurotic." Perhaps Pier set him off by telling him that she had decided (or was being forced by her mother) to marry Vic Damone. Perhaps he had discovered that Marlon Brando, who was also one of Pier's admirers, was a frequent visitor to the Pierangeli house in Brentwood.

Pier's marriage to Vic Damone broke up in a storm of recriminations. She fled with their son, Perry (named after friend Perry Como), to Italy. Several years later, she was so broke she agreed to let Damone bring Perry back to California. Then she married another musician, Armando Trovajoli, and had another son, Andrew. This marriage fell apart, too, and the Italian courts awarded custody of seven-year-old Andrew to Trovajoli.

Abandoned and nearly penniless, she came back to Hollywood in 1970 and shared an apartment with Helena Sorrell, a former drama coach. The only work she could find was in an X-rated film, *Love Me, Love My Wife*. She lost a role (wife of one of the sons) in *The Godfather* that might have revived her career. "Too old," the producers told her agent.

She developed stomach trouble. She began taking pills for the pain. One night she took too many. The coroner's verdict was death by overdose. After Jimmy's death, years earlier, she had said: "He was the love of my youth—perhaps my greatest love."

NINE

Occasionally, in the months that followed the filming of
East of Eden, Jimmy would fly back to New York. Like
so many actors who have received "the fatal call to Hollywood," he was determined to return to New York after
each picture to get back into what he called "life and
the living of it."

He would stay for several days, or several weeks, living in the fifth-floor walk-up (19 West Sixty-eighth
Street) he had rented before leaving for Los Angeles,
and then, as mysteriously as he had appeared, he would
disappear, dropping everything and everybody.

He loved to make surprise entrances in people's lives.
He would show up at photographer Roy Schatt's studio
and ask for a lesson with the camera. He would knock at
composer Lenny Rosenman's door and ask for an hour at
the piano. He would badger Eartha Kitt into taking him
along to one of her modern dance classes.

Sometimes he stayed home and banged on his bongos,
or sketched, or listened to records. Sometimes he dragged

his bongos up and down Third Avenue bars, putting on noisy unscheduled performances until he got kicked out. Sometimes he sat quietly playing chess in a corner of Jerry's Bar on Fifty-fourth Street.

On one warm fall evening, he drifted into a double date with Tye Morrow, an actor he had met while he was still doing TV bits. "Jimmy and I," Morrow remembers, "went to an impromptu party, which means it just started. It was on Fifty-third Street. There was a fella, an artist, a good old soul, named Arthur Jacobs, who used to have an apartment on the south side of West Fifty-third Street, right across from the Rehearsal Club. Well, we bought some beer, and there were about two or three or four gals from the Rehearsal Club and Arthur and Jimmy and I, and I play a harmonica, so Jimmy got his bongos and I got the harmonica, and Arthur played the Coca-Cola bottles—and we all drank beer and had a ball.

"And I recall this night that Jimmy and I—we had known these girls before, you know—we took two of the gals and we said, well—it was real late, about two o'clock in the morning—let's get some beer and we'll go up to my place or your place and have a ball. And Jimmy says, 'I got some crazy records. Let's go up to my place, I've got some real great stuff.' And the type of stuff that he had was the Les Baxter kind of thing, voodoo beat, the African-beat. So we got a cab, Jimmy and these two lovely—actually, they were very nice gals—we stopped off and got some beer. And we got up to his place, it was almost an attic, and we tiptoed up the stairs and walked in—and the girls had never been there before and they couldn't believe it. I could see their faces, they couldn't believe it—he had opened a can of pork and beans or something which looked like he had opened it two months back because a few spoonfuls had been taken out and it was covered with almost like spider webs. The green had formed across the top and it was still sitting in the exact same place with the spoon there. They couldn't believe it, and there were piles of clothes on the floor. So I said, let's get this stuff up.

"What were we going to drink beer from? He had no glasses. He had a Silex. He made coffee in the john on a little burner he had back there. So he took this Silex, plugged it up with a cork, because one of the gals says, I'm not going to drink out of the bottle. He washed it out, put a cork in the bottom, and poured the beer. We got those big quart bottles and Jimmy and I, of course, were drinking out of the bottle. One of the gals was holding that Silex. 'Well,' she said, 'this is a treat.' And he had a big bed with a big shag rug next to it. The rug was white and kind of dirty. And he would always say, 'Come on, Tye, 'scuse us, girls!' and we'd go out, the hall was right there in the end of the room, really, and we'd flip a coin, heads or tails. One would get the bed and the other would get the shag rug.

"At any rate, this night he got the bed. Now don't misunderstand. I'm not saying that we went in for indiscriminate sex in front of everybody and his brother. The lights would go off until you couldn't see your hand in front of your face. So, the gal and I are sitting on the shag rug, actually leaning against the bed, and Jimmy and the other gal are on the bed and they're smooching it up as we are, feeling about, and the music is playing and we're talking back and forth, but then, all of a sudden, the conversation stops, and nothing is said for a considerable period of time, and then, right out of the blue and right at the most inopportune moment—I would say twenty minutes had passed, with no sound and no conversation— now what he was doing I have no idea—but he popped up with, 'Hey, Tye, you got your finger in yet?' And then he went, 'Ugh, ugh, ugh,' and I came back with something like, 'How uncouth! How crude can you get?' And some- times we'd do this until daybreak.

"And then, generally, well, I know on this occasion, something like seven or seven thirty—at any rate, the dawn was up—this one gal and I, I took her back to the Rehearsal Club and the other gal stayed up there for a little while. And I saw her later, the gal that stayed with Jimmy, I saw her a little bit later that evening, and she says, 'You know, nothing happened up there.' And I said, 'I didn't ask you whether anything happened or not.' But she—she's this type of gal—she said nothing happened. And I said, 'Aw, come on, aw.' Couple of days later, I saw her again and she said, 'You know, he hasn't called me or anything. I expected him to. I like him.' But I doubt if he ever saw her again. I don't think he ever did."

On several of his New York visits, Jimmy dropped in to observe at the Actors Studio. He had stopped trying out work there himself after Lee Strasberg criticized a scene he presented. "I don't know what's inside me," he told Bill Bast after that experience. "I don't know what happens when I act—inside. But if I let them dissect me like a rabbit in a clinical research laboratory, I might not be able to produce again. For Chrissake, they might sterilize me!"

Jimmy wanted to act in New York. He wanted to do another play on Broadway (and by this time he could have landed a star part), but the availability clause in his Warner's contract made it impossible to go up for anything involving a long run. The contract did, however, permit one-night stands on TV. Jane Deacy got him a lead in *I Am a Fool,* a "General Electric Theatre" drama in which he played with Eddie Albert and a then unknown young actress named Natalie Wood.

TEN

In the early part of the new year (1955), Jimmy was in New York enjoying the anonymity that the sneak previews of *East of Eden* had now made impossible on the coast. On February 8, he was twenty-four. On February 27, Warner Brothers ran a big ad in the New York *Times* that was the beginning of the end of his invisibility in New York: "March 10th—ASTOR, B'way at 45th St. ELIA KAZAN—JOHN STEINBECK—AND THE 'SOMETHING' THAT MEANS 'EVERYTHING' IN MOTION PICTURE GREATNESS! Ask anybody—EAST OF EDEN is Steinbeck's masterpiece. Its sons and lovers, its saints and sinners, its losers and winners all have the look of, and the yen for, life. If these bone-raw, flesh-real people stormed almost bodily off Steinbeck's electric pages, you can imagine what happens to them in the hands of Elia Kazan, who just about *invented* screen realism as it is known today. EAST OF EDEN is one for the book—the one where they keep all the records of all the awards!" Jimmy peers nearsightedly, romantically, out of a half-tone captioned: "This is James Dean—a very special new star!"

In addition to an impressive advertising campaign, Warner Brothers was planning a special celebrity preview at the Astor Theatre on the evening of March 9, 1955 (the official public opening was March 10). The preview was announced as a benefit for the Actors Studio. Dozens of Broadway and Hollywood celebrities attended. Marilyn Monroe handed out programs.

For Jimmy, Hollywood was coming to New York—in force. The day before the preview, he called Jane Deacy: "I'm sorry, Mom," he said (he called both Ortense Winslow and Jane Deacy "Mom"), "but you know I can't make this scene. I can't handle it. I'm going back to the Coast tonight."

So, without the presence of its "very special new star," *East of Eden* opened.

In the New York *Times*, Bosley Crowther was picky and peevish. "Only a small part of John Steinbeck's 'East of Eden' has been used in the motion picture version of it that Elia Kazan has done, and it is questionable whether that part contains the best of the book . . . Yet Mr. Kazan has at it . . . with such elaborate pictorial build-up and such virtuosity on his actors' part that he gets across the illusion of a drama more pregnant than it is . . . But the stubborn fact is that the people who move about in the film are not sufficiently well established to give point to the anguish through which they go, and the demonstrations of their torment are perceptibly stylized and grotesque. Especially is this true of James Dean in the role of Cal. This young actor, who is here doing his first big screen stint, is a mass of histrionic gingerbread. He scuffs his feet, he whirls, he pouts, he sputters, he leans against walls, he rolls his eyes, he swallows his words, he ambles slack-kneed—all like Marlon Brando used to do. Never have we seen a performer so clearly follow another's style. Mr. Kazan should be spanked for permitting him to do such a sophomoric thing. Whatever there might be of reasonable torment in this youngster is buried beneath the clumsy display."

William K. Zinsser in the New York *Herald Tribune*, said, less testily: "He (Jimmy) will inevitably be compared to Marlon Brando, for Kazan has stamped him with the same hesitant manner of speech, the same blind groping for love and security that he gave Brando in 'On the Waterfront.' But if the performances are akin, so are the roles, and to complain about the similarity would be quibbling . . . Everything about Dean suggests the lonely, misunderstood nineteen-year-old. Even from a distance you know a lot about him by the way he walks—with his hands in his pockets and his head down, slinking like a dog waiting for a bone. When he talks, he stammers and pauses, uncertain of what he is trying to say. When he listens, he is full of restless energy—he stretches, he rolls on the ground, he chins himself on the porch railing, like a small boy impatient of his elders' chatter . . . Occasionally, he smiles unaccountably as if at some dark joke known only to him. 'He scares me,' his brother's girl, Abra (Julie Harris), keeps saying with reason. You sense the loneliness in him. But you also like him . . . 'East of

Eden,'" Zinsser concludes, "has the look of truth. It also has a wistful beauty and a great deal of power. It pulls no punches."

In his Sunday follow-up review (*Herald Tribune*, March 13, 1955), Zinsser seems to have grown even fonder of Jimmy: "In every little mannerism, as well as in the things he says, Dean shapes this secretive character, rather like Hamlet in many ways, and we finally feel that we know him at least as well as his father does."

Time magazine's review (March 21, 1955) bordered on a rave: "The picture is brilliant entertainment and more than that, it announces a new star, James Dean, whose prospects look as bright as any young actor's since Marlon Brando . . . Dean, a young man from Indiana, is unquestionably the biggest news Hollywood has made in 1955. Dean, like Julie Harris, Marlon Brando, Eva Marie Saint and most of the young people Kazan uses, is a product of the Actors Studio, something known as 'the tilted-pelvis' school of *naturalistic acting*. Like so many Studio students, who have been brought up on 'the Stanislavsky Method,' Dean tries so hard to find the part in himself that he often forgets to put himself into the part. But no matter what he is doing, he has the presence of a young lion and the same sense of danger about him. His eye is as empty as an animal's, and he lolls and gallops with the innocence and grace of an animal. Then, occasionally, he flicks a sly little look that seems to say: 'Well, all this is human, too—or had you forgotten?'"

The *Newsweek* piece was both review and interview. "'East of Eden' is a somber mood piece that may break no box-office records. But it will be received gratefully by anyone with more than an escapist interest in the screen . . . Like Marlon Brando, Jimmy Dean approached Hollywood with a pronounced indifference to dress and manners. He wore shabby sport shirts, faded blue jeans, a leather jacket. He rode a motorcycle to work. He loves to play music (piano, bongo drums, recorder) and read books (as many as six at a time, he claims).

"When Hollywood labeled him a victim of 'Brandoism' —a malady observable in at least a dozen stage and television actors—Dean was not at all upset. 'People,' he said, 'were telling me I behaved like Brando before I know who Brando was. I am not disturbed by the comparison, nor am I flattered. I have my own personal rebellion and don't have to rely on Brando's . . .' Dean, who is an athletic 5 foot 8, acquired a horse—a palomino named Cisco—soon after he landed in Hollywood. Now, in addition to the motorcycle, he has a German sports car (mostly, a friend explains, because 'girls wouldn't ride on his motorcycle'). He also has picked up more than a normal ration of cocksureness. 'I'm a serious-minded and intense little devil,' he says of himself, 'terribly gauche and so tense that I don't see how people stay in the same room with me. I know I wouldn't tolerate myself.' Asked how he liked Hollywood, Dean said, 'Geographical location means nothing to me and neither did coming out to Hollywood. A man can produce no matter where the hell he is.'"

One of the trade papers, *The Hollywood Reporter*, summed it all up in down-to-business, theatre-manager language: "QUALITY FILM BASED ON THE STEINBECK NOVEL. EXCELLENT PRODUCTION, ACTING AND DIRECTION. INTRODUCING JAMES DEAN WHO MAY BE A HYPO AT THE BOX OFFICE."

Hedda Hopper did an about face and began to crank out paragraphs of praise for the new star. "HEDDA HOPPER'S HOLLYWOOD, 702 Guaranty Building, Hollywood, 28, California. For Release Sunday, March 27, 1955. JAMES DEAN: I can't remember when any screen newcomer generated as much excitement in Hollywood as did James Dean in his first picture, 'East of Eden.'

"Word got out that we had a 'young genius' in our midst who was as rebellious as he was talented. Producers, directors, critics flocked to see the film before its release. Inevitably, they found their attention, despite the fine work of the other actors, riveted on a 23-year-old farm boy from Indiana . . . I had seen Dean only once, slumped, surly looking and carelessly dressed in a studio commissary. He was not impressive. But after watching his performance, I admit he was worth all the praise given him—and perhaps more . . . Wanting to know what made him tick, I invited him to my house for a chat. He arrived on the dot, wearing a charcoal colored suit, black shirt and tie, and on his feet, heavy riding boots. When you see him on the screen you are not aware that he is not quite six feet tall. His height is a sore spot with him. Ask him how tall he is and he'll retort: 'My feet just touch the ground! Abe Lincoln said that, I didn't.' A serious, thoughtful and amazingly articulate youngster, he takes you by surprise with unexpected flashes of humor."

Later, in her book, *The Whole Truth and Nothing But,* Hedda described that first meeting again, but by then the Jimmy myth had gilded her vision of reality. This time, Clifton Webb and Jack Warner are involved and Jimmy has on his Brando-hero suit and fondles a gift from Elizabeth Taylor. Listen now, as we rejoin Hedda in Hollywood: "When an invitation came to see the preview of 'East of Eden,' nobody could have dragged me there. But I heard the next day from Clifton Webb, whose judgement I respect: 'last night I saw one of the most extraordinary performances of my life. Get the studio to run that movie over for you. You'll be crazy about this boy Jimmy Dean.'

" 'I've seen him,' I said coldly.

" 'Forget it—I read your piece. Just watch him in this picture.'

"In the projection room I sat spellbound. I couldn't remember ever having seen a young man with such power, so many facets of expression, so much sheer invention as this actor. I telephoned Jack Warner. 'I'd like to talk with your Mr. Dean. He may not want to do an interview with me. If he doesn't, I shan't hold it against him. But I'd love to have him come over to my house.'

"Within minutes, his reaction was passed back to me: 'He'll be delighted.' A day or so later he rang my doorbell, spic and span in black pants and black leather jacket, though his hair was tousled and he wore a pair of heavy boots that a deep-sea diver wouldn't have sneezed at. He carried a silver St. Genesius medal that Liz Taylor had given him, holding it as we talked."

It was a whole year after *Eden* that Jimmy worked with Elizabeth Taylor (in the film *Giant*). Perhaps Hedda really meant to say Pier Angeli, or perhaps she didn't. By the time Hedda's book came out, Pier Angeli's career was in trouble, but Liz Taylor's was still big business.

Linkage is the principal tool used in star making and star maintenance: the name of a rising star is linked to the name of an already established star, the title of a new film is linked to the name of its already famous actors, or more rarely to the name of its already renowned director (Hitchcock, Truffaut, Fellini, Bergman). Links must be forged between the unknown and the known, even if they have to be invented. Hedda Hopper knew her job and she did it well.

With New York and Hollywood safely on the Dean bandwagon, Warner Brothers began to invite Middle America aboard. On April 4, 1955, Adeline Nall, Jimmy's high school drama and speech teacher, got the following telegram:

DEA190 OB535
O.BNA443 NL-WUX BURBANK CALIF. 4-
MISS ADELINE NALL-
FAIRMONT (SIC) HIGH SCHOOL FAIRMONT IND-
WOULD BE HONORED IF YOU WOULD ACCEPT THIS
WIRE AS INVITATION TO ATTEND SPECIAL SCREENING
OF MY NEW WARNER BROS PICTURE "EAST OF EDEN"
AT INDIANA STATE THEATRE MARION APRIL 5 10:00
AM. ALTHOUGH PICTURE OPENS APRIL 10 WOULD

LIKE YOU TO BE ONE OF THE FIRST PERSONS FROM
GRANT COUNTY TO SEE IT. SINCERELY-
YOUR FORMER PUPIL JAMES DEAN

The Marion *Chronicle-Tribune* had the story before
Adeline Nall had the telegram. On Sunday, April 3, under
a picture of Jimmy struggling with Raymond Massey, it
said: "HIGH SCHOOL DRAMATICS TEACHER WHO TAUGHT JAMES
DEAN TO BE GUEST AT PREVIEW OF PICTURE."

On April 6, the Marion *Chronicle-Times* reported:
"'EAST OF EDEN' STAR PRAISED BY TEACHER. 'It was beyond
all we had expected,' Mrs. Adeline Mart Nall, Fairmount
High School speech teacher, said Tuesday of the performance by her former student, James Dean, in Warner
Brothers' 'East of Eden.' . . . 'It didn't seem strange at all
to watch Jim work in this fine movie,' Mrs. Nall said. 'All
of us felt we were right there with him. Many of the
movements of 'Cal Trask' were characteristic movements
of James Dean,' she continued. 'His funny little laugh,
which ripples with the slightest provocation; his quick,
jerky, springy walks and actions; his sudden change from
frivolity to gloom—all were just like Jim used to do,' Mrs.
Nall said. . . . "Relatives of the Fairmount youth who
were among the 200 persons attending the special screening at the Indiana Theatre Tuesday morning were Mr.
and Mrs. Marcus Winslow (Uncle Marcus and Aunt
Ortense), and son (Markie Jr.), Mrs. Marvin Reese Pea-
cock (Joanne Winslow), Mr. and Mrs. Charles Dean
(Jimmy's paternal grandparents), Mr. and Mrs. Charles
Nolan Dean (Charlie Nolan was Jimmy's favorite

uncle), Mrs. Leon Moon, Mrs. Worth Moon, John Wilson (Jimmy's maternal grandfather), Mrs. Clarence Ballinger, Howard Wilson and Anna Wilson."

The home-town paper, the Fairmount *News* (April 7, 1955), front-paged the story: "DEAN'S 'EDEN' PROVES TO BE POWERFUL." Other Indiana papers crowed: "FAIRMOUNT TEACHER INSPIRED PUPIL TO STARDOM!" . . . "FAIRMOUNT'S BOY IS GOING PLACES" . . . "EX-FARM BOY NOW IS MAKING HAY IN MOVIES."

ELEVEN

But Jimmy was not in Fairmount collecting laurels; he was back in Hollywood spending the days getting ready to shoot *Rebel Without a Cause* and the nights hanging out with two friends he had acquired shortly after breaking up with Pier Angeli. One was Jack Simmons, an aspiring actor, and the other was Maila Nurmi, a beautiful young woman, who, as Vampira, hostessed a TV "Horror Movie Show."

Simmons has since become a rather mysterious Los Angeles real estate operator—he is said to have provided Andy Warhol and Paul Morrisey with the Hollywood mansion in their film, *Heat*. Maila Nurmi eventually opened an antique shop called Vampira's Attic.

She first met Jimmy at Googie's, a hamburger joint (now called Steak 'n Stein) next to Schwab's: "I had met Jack Simmons the night before at a premiere. Someone brought Jack over to me and introduced him to me and I said to Jack, 'You know, this is remarkable, because I came here for the express purpose of seeing who in Hollywood

I wanted to know and I selected two people, one of whom was you, and then you were just brought to me as if, you know, a gift on wings. Randy didn't know I wanted to know you. And there's one other person here I want to know. But he's gone now. He was Terry Moore's date."

Dick Clayton, who agented for both Jimmy and Terry, had arranged the date to produce a photo suitable for magazine and newspaper release. It shows the supposedly romantic pair—Jimmy looking genuinely uncomfortable—emerging from a limousine in front of the theatre.

The next day, Jack and Maila were lunching at Googie's, when Jimmy Dean arrived on the scene. Jack got up and brought him over. "Jimmy," remembers Maila, "acknowledged the introduction and I got right to the nitty gritty. Instead of saying, 'How do you do?' I said, 'Where is she?' Psychically, I knew him before I even met him, so I didn't waste words: 'Where is she?' He said, 'Who?' And I said, 'Your mother'; and he made a whooshing sound, reddened, and threw his arms over his head.

"And so then immediately, he said, 'I want you to come to my apartment. I want to read a poem to you.' And it was actually a Ray Bradbury short story about a boy who hanged himself, a boy who had a close relationship with his mother. So he read the story to me. He was on Sunset Plaza Drive then, the little place above a garage that he described as a wastebasket with walls.

"I found it disconcerting—his fascination with that story, because I felt it was his own suicide he was talking about. When I asked him, 'Where is she?'—his mother—and he said, 'She cut out,' I tried to get to the bottom of it: 'What do you mean, she cut out?' 'Well,' he said, 'she, you know, left, she died.' I asked, 'She killed herself, or she died?' 'Well,' he said, 'yes, she committed suicide, in a sense.' Intellectually, he knew she had died, but emotionally, he felt that she had abandoned him.

"So then he told me the circumstances of his mother's death and how he had been orphaned at nine and how, when he was going to lean on his father—since he was an only child and devoted to his mother and father both, and a tender poet, his mother had named him after Lord Byron and he was close to Mama and when she like cut out, as he felt, then of course, he turned to father who was distant and cool and disciplined and all that—he turned to father and father gave him away!"

Jimmy, Maila, and Jack began meeting every evening at midnight: "We'd coffee-klatsch about—Googie's, Schwab's, Banney's Beanery, the little coffee shops. It was chatter. I guess we wanted to share the experience we'd had in the course of the day, as you do when you like someone, feel close to someone. I think it was rather adolescent. And Jack Simmons was always with us. We were never alone."

Jimmy tried very hard to get Jack Simmons what eventually turned out to be the Sal Mineo part (Plato) in *Rebel Without a Cause*. In Maila Nurmi's opinion: "They wrote that part about Jack. I don't know if they admit it. I had the impression that Sal Mineo in that picture was Jack Simmons as I knew him at that time. Jimmy wanted—well, Jack was always hanging out—the three of us together, Jimmy and Jack and I—and Jimmy was work-

ing and I was working, but Jack wasn't. He was an un-
employed busboy at the time. And I said, "This isn't really
right. Jack has got to be working, too—we can't just hand
him bits of, you know, pick up his tab and hand him
money for his room rent. So he should be working."

Jimmy arranged a screen test for Jack. It was shot on
the old *Streetcar Named Desire* set. Jimmy and Jack were
supposed to laugh hysterically in inappropriate reaction
to a terrifying incident. Jack wasn't sure he would be able
to laugh. Jimmy took him behind the set, unzipped, and
began to pee, seeing how high he could make the stream
go, pretending to aim it at the camera. Jack began to
laugh hysterically. They went right into the scene.

But Jack did not get the part. Director Ray and script
writer Stern found his acting too mannered.

"Anyway," continues Maila Nurmi, "one Thanksgiving
afternoon—sometimes we also met in the afternoon, but
never by given appointment, we just waited for one
another at Googie's—I arrived at Googie's, about four
o'clock, wearing white sailor pants. In those days, women
didn't wear white sailor pants—today, it's not unusual—
but I was married through all this and I was wearing my
husband's white sailor pants. So a little while later,
Jimmy arrived wearing white sailor pants and, of course,
it was not seasonal, either. It was November. Anyway, we
both had them. I had never worn them before and he
hadn't worn them in the period of our acquaintance. So
we both happened to be wearing white sailor pants on
the very same day. And I had three upper front teeth
missing—well, he had three front teeth missing, too, but

one over—and as he came in I noticed that his bridge-work was missing. So before he saw me, I took my bridge-work out and hid it. And I didn't say anything about it, but then he noticed that we were both wearing white sailor pants and we both had our bridgework missing. And we laughed, and that was adolescent, but those are the kinds of things we did. So then he said, 'I broke mine on the turkey.' So I pretended to have lost mine the same way.

"And the three of us would drive around. We didn't go far. We had Jack's little car, an old car that shimmied a lot in the back. We'd go to drive-ins maybe, to Tiny Naylor's. It was very like when I was in high school and going to the local drugstore, except that I was with someone with whom I could see the world in unison. I mean, I had someone who understood how I was seeing the world. And he had a delicious sense of humor. His social satire was marvelous. He used to draw cartoons.

"I think he did Charlie Tuna, for example. I think he created him. I had a friend named Geraldine Bogdana-vic who was Star-Kist Tuna—her family was Star-Kist Tuna. And one day Geraldine said to me, 'Oh, it's terrible—all those poor fishermen and their wives and their babies, not eating because of the sardine strike.' And I said, 'Geraldine, in the eye of God, any anonymous Geraldine Bogdanavic is no more valuable than .any anonymous sardine.'

"She didn't know what that meant, it was just a little irritating, but I told it to Jimmy and so he drew—that night when he was drawing—a picture of a fish, on a wharf, fishing, and he was catching a Geraldine. And I got it and I gave it to Geraldine. And the fish had clothes on, he was catching a people, he caught a Geraldine Bogdanavic who was a mermaid. And Geraldine gave this to her brother-in-law who was the head of Star-Kist Tuna and after that, Charlie Tuna emerged—so I really think Jimmy did it. His drawing looked just like Charlie Tuna."

After bopping around at these late-night kiddie klatsches with Maila and Jack, Jimmy would wake up in the morning to a world that was beginning to treat him like an important person. Jack Warner, his right-hand man Steve Trilling, and other Warner executives had gotten the message *East of Eden*'s sneak-preview audiences were sending: *You have a big new star on your hands!*

Another young-man-in-terrible-trouble project was in the works at the studio, but no one had yet thought of James Dean for the part. The studio had optioned Robert Lindner's book, *Rebel Without a Cause*, and Jack Warner had assigned Nicholas Ray to direct. Ray saw the studio's offer as his chance to get his own pet project onto the screen. He first called it *The Blind Run*.

The outline establishes a trio of kids: Demo, Jimmy, and Eve. Demo is initiated into Jimmy's gang by the ordeal of a "blind run": two cars with lights out racing toward each other from opposite ends of a tunnel. Miraculously, the cars miss each other. But then, Demo, angered that his mother and father refuse to attend a party he and Jimmy and Eve have planned for all their parents, steals a car and stomps a man to death. Later, he tells Jimmy and Eve: "It was like killing my old man." Demo is caught, tried and sentenced to death. Later, Jimmy is killed in a gang fight, leaving a pregnant Eve to watch his body being ambulanced away.

Ray knew that much of his outline needed changing; but one idea he was determined not to change. "It should be kept in mind that the youth is always in the foreground and adults are, for the most part, shown only as kids see them."

He first hired Leon Uris and sent him scurrying around Los Angeles to talk to police officers, social workers, psychiatrists, and delinquents. But for all the down-to-earth interviews the writer conducted, the script soon began to take on epic proportions. It was becoming, Uris style, the history of an entire community, old people, young people, everybody—exactly what Ray did not want. Another writer was brought in, ex-schoolteacher Irving Shulman, who knew something about the kids' point of view and who, it also happened, was crazy about sports cars, the passionate preoccupation of James Dean, the young actor Ray had recently brought into the project.

(Just a few weeks earlier, Jimmy had purchased a $4,000 Porsche Speedster and entered a road race in Palm Springs, where he took first place in the amateur class and, even more surprisingly, third place in the professional class. Ken Miles, a driver who sometimes competed against Jimmy, says: "Dean might have gone on to become a very good racer. But the odds were against his becoming a great one. I'll tell you why.

"Most people have the idea that sports car racing is principally a matter of speed. It isn't. Speed is a factor, certainly, but this kind of racing is primarily a test of the driver's skill. How cleverly can he maneuver his car at high speed in and out of a pack of other cars, all with drivers who are attempting to maneuver their cars at high speed.

"To win such a race, a man must, of necessity, throw away courtesy and any inherent feeling he may have for another man's safety. This is the risk, a rather strange kind of sportsmanship, that every racer accepts.

"Dean was always too careful with other drivers. He didn't care about his own neck, but he would not take any risk involving another driver. You can't win races that way.

"Jimmy wanted speed. He wanted his body to hurtle across over the ground, the faster the better. Jimmy was a straightaway driver. His track was the shortest distance between here and there.")

Jimmy could talk about cars by the hour. Director Ray figured he could count on a lot of automotive rapport between his writer and his star.

Shulman made important contributions to the story. He cut out the "blind run," and put in the "chickie run" (the boy who jumps out of his car last before it hurtles over a cliff wins the machismo trial). He also developed the principal characters: Jim, Judy, and Plato. But Ray wanted Plato to be shot down at the planetarium, where the "end of the world" had been shown earlier to Plato's high school class. This, Ray thought, would frame the particular tragedy of Plato's death in one more universal. Shulman didn't buy that. But Jimmy and his friend, Leonard Rosenman, who had been hired to write the music, went along with Ray on the planetarium idea. So Shulman dropped out.

Ray next hired Stewart Stern, whom Jimmy had first run into at Arthur Loew Jr.'s house (Stern and Loew are cousins). Stewart and Jimmy spent the first minutes of that chance meeting imitating animal cries, each having perfected his own assortment of moos, caws, and chirps. This provided them with far more rapport than sports cars.

Stern wrote the final *Rebel* screenplay in little more than a month, demonstrating a remarkable ability to withstand the insane last-minute-before-production pressures which director Ray, star Dean, and producer Weisbard were exerting on him to conjure sunbursts of clarity out of their murky after-hours inspirations.

Here is Warner Brothers' synopsis of the story as filmed:

REBEL WITHOUT A CAUSE

A man, beaten up by some teen-age toughs, is left lying unconscious in the street. Jim (JAMES DEAN), an unruly youth questioned by the police, is released for lack of evidence, but not before revealing a disrespect for his domineering mother (ANN DORAN) and weakling father (JIM

BACKUS). With Judy (NATALIE WOOD), a girl
friend, and his pal Plato (SAL MINEO), Jim tries
to join a gang led by Buzz (COREY ALLEN). Instead, Jim and Buzz wind up fighting a knife
duel and agree to meet later for a test whereby
the boys each get into a hot rod, drive the cars
toward the edge of a cliff and leap out seconds
before the vehicles tumble to the jagged rocks
below. Both boys racing at breakneck speed, the
cliff's edge looming ahead, Buzz reaches for the
door, but his jacket sleeve hooks over the handle. Trapped, he and the car spin through the
air to a violent death below. Fearing Jim will go
to the police, Buzz's friends track him to a deserted mansion where he, Judy, and Plato,
armed with his father's gun, are hiding out. Plato
opens fire, killing one of the youths. Summoned
by the shots, police close in and order the gun-
crazed youngster to surrender. Plato makes a
furtive move mistaken by a policeman who fires
at him. Jim, saddened by his buddy's death, is
comforted by his parents. From this experience,
they have come to understand one another.

Nicholas Ray had seen Jimmy in *East of Eden* and had
met him later on the Warner lot. He was certain at once
that he had found "the ideal actor for Jim Stark," but he
worried about working with such a temperamental performer. "One side of the difficulty was personal," Ray
said later. "Since beginning to know him a little, I had
realized that, for a successful collaboration, he needed

a special kind of climate. He needed reassurance, tolerance, understanding. An important way of creating this
was to involve him at every stage in the development of
the picture."

Ray certainly believed what he was saying, but it was
also a face-saving way of explaining that Jimmy took advantage of the power his growing reputation had given
him. According to Lenny Rosenman, Maila Nurmi and
Jim Backus, who played his father in the film, Jimmy became, in fact, co-director of *Rebel Without a Cause*.

Unlike Kazan, who was at the top of the heap, Ray
needed Jimmy. He considered himself lucky to get a
hot new star for a movie the studio insisted on treating
like a "B" picture (even though, eventually, according to
Variety's list of all-time box-office champs, it grossed
almost as much, $4,600,000, as "A" picture *East of Eden*,
$5,000,000, and, because of its lower budget, made the
studio more profit). Warner Brothers, accurately seismo-
graphing the earthquake of Jimmy's popularity, would
probably never have put him into *Rebel* at all if *Giant*,
his next "A" picture, had not been delayed. George
Stevens was waiting for Elizabeth Taylor to become
available after the birth of a baby (Christopher Edward
Wilding).

Jimmy, who was beginning to think he might want
to become a director, enjoyed his unusual position on
Rebel. He did not hesitate to force his ideas into the story.
He would sit long evenings with Ray working over the
script. He did not hesitate, either, to throw his weight
around on the set. Before shooting the scene in Juvenile

Hall which called for him to bang his fist on a desk, deliver a loud, angry monologue, and provoke a fight with the youth officer, Jimmy kept the cast and crew waiting for an hour. He sat in his dressing room with the lights off, drinking red wine and listening to the *"Ride of the Valkyries"* turned up full blast. When the rest of the cast was about to fall apart, he charged out onto the set, did the whole monologue in one take, and did it so convincingly that the members of the crew, angry as they were, could not help applauding.

Jimmy understood the differences between stage acting and film acting. On stage, an actor has a chance to sustain character, to build moments, to climb toward the climax of a drama that usually progresses chronologically and is actually performed in a continuous time period of only two or three hours. On a movie set, an actor is asked to jump right into the middle of even the most explosive scenes, and the performance is spread out over weeks and months. Most often, too, the story is shot out of sequence.

Each scene is represented by a strip of colored cardboard. The strips are organized on a long panel: day scenes with day scenes, night scenes with night scenes, scenes in a certain location with other scenes in the same location, even though they may be at opposite ends of the script. Sometimes, when an important actor can only be present for the first, middle, or last weeks of the shooting schedule, all of his or her scenes will be bunched together, regardless of location or light considerations. The resulting sequence solves budget problems, logistical problems, career problems, union problems; but it has nothing to do with reinforcing the flow of the story. Somehow, the director and the actors are expected to overcome this difficulty.

Before shooting began, Ray got Jimmy and Jim Backus together to work through the script. Scene by scene, they rehearsed dialogue, argued out the motivations of their characters. To help keep the story alive while shooting, Ray scheduled as many scenes in story sequence as the budget would allow. And Jimmy, although he obviously couldn't spend an hour getting high on wine and Wagner before every take, made sure he always got in at least ten minutes deep concentration before walking out in front of the cameras. He would try to fly walk a wall, or shadow box, or scramble up one of the long studio ladders. When he had worked himself into character, he would signal Ray and the scene would begin.

Throughout the film, Jimmy insisted on realism. Doubles were never used. When the script called for a knife fight, he and Corey Allen (the actor playing Buzz) did the scene themselves with real switchblades. Jimmy was so agile that Mushy Callahan, an ex-pug who served as trainer and technical adviser for the fight scenes, thought Jimmy could have become a champion in his weight class if he had wanted a career in boxing.

He weighed only 140 pounds, but he was strong. In a scene in which he gets into an argument with his father, he had to pull 200-pound Jim Backus down the stairs, drag him across the room, throw him into a chair, and then, as the chair toppled over, leap on top of him and try to choke him. As Ray covered the action from every angle—close-ups, long shots, overheads, up-from-unders, Jimmy dragged and carried Backus down the stairs, across the room, and into the chair time after time without bruising or even frightening him.

During a scene at the old mansion (the same one used in *Sunset Boulevard* and rented for *Rebel* from its owner, oil billionaire J. Paul Getty at $200 a week) Jimmy and Natalie Wood, who played Judy, slip into a skit in which they pretend to be a married couple looking for a place to live. Sal Mineo, who played Plato, takes on the role of real estate agent.

JUDY

There's just one thing. What about—

PLATO

Children? Well, we don't really
encourage them. They're so noisy and
troublesome, don't you agree?

JUDY

Yes. And so terribly annoying when
they cry. I just don't know what to
do when they cry, do you dear?

JIM

Of course. Drown them like puppies.

In going over the script, Jimmy had decided to punch up the "Drown them like puppies" line by doing it in the voice of Jim Backus' cartoon character, Mr. Magoo. "Evidently," says Backus, "word sifted up to the office, and some executive came down to the set and said, 'I hear you're going to do Mr. Magoo.' And Jimmy said, 'Yeah, I guess I am.' 'Well,' says the executive, 'as long as you're going to do it would you mind making it Bugs Bunny?—Because that's a Warner property.' Jimmy just stared at him."

"And another time, I'll never forget," says Backus, "Jimmy and I were walking down the street, a studio street, and Jack Warner is standing there with two obviously very important distributors or exhibitors. And evidently, as we approached, you could see that Jack was saying to them, 'See, coming down the street is the kid that's just absolutely . . . *East of Eden* . . . and the whole thing . . . and now he's making . . . and then he's going into *Giant*.' And Jimmy, as he came up alongside—Jack was resplendent in an iridescent suit of some kind—and Jimmy went up to him and said: 'Have it cleaned and burned!'"

Jimmy pushed himself mercilessly, on the set and off. When his old Indiana school pal, Whitey Rust, arrived for a visit, Jimmy took him out driving and drinking night after night. Often they didn't get back to Jimmy's place on Sunset Plaza Drive until four or five in the morning. Whitey would sleep until noon, but somehow Jimmy would always manage to get himself out of bed at daybreak and drive to the studio.

Whitey found his friend Jimmy little changed from the days when they played together in Uncle Marcus' barn. On first arriving in Los Angeles, Whitey had gone straight to the studio. There was a pass waiting for him at the gate. As he came onto the set, Jimmy, who was between takes, spotted him, threw his hands up toward the ceiling of the gigantic sound stage and yelled: "Hold a hell of a lot of hay, wouldn't she, Whitey?"

By June, the filming of *Rebel* was finished. Jimmy, with hardly a day off to catch his breath, was put into *Giant*.

TWELVE

Screenwriters Fred Guiol and Ivan Moffat managed to get Edna Ferber's big 447-page Texas tale into a 178-page script that was final on April 4, 1955 The studio campaign book summed up the film story this way:

GIANT

Bick Benedict (ROCK HUDSON), the young owner of a half-million-acre cattle ranch in Texas, comes to Maryland to buy a magnificent black stallion. He meets, falls in love with and quickly marries Leslie (ELIZABETH TAYLOR). Though they are much in love, there are many clashes of temperament at their vast Reata Ranch, so different from Leslie's home in Maryland. Leslie is shocked at the status of the Mexican ranch hands who are underpaid and underprivileged. She takes matters into her own hands by giving them medical care. A stubborn spinster, Bick's sister, Luz (MERCEDES MC CAMBRIDGE), runs the house. Her unreasonable rule over the

Reata Ranch is ended when she is killed in a fall while riding. In her will, she leaves a small piece of her land to Jett Rink (JAMES DEAN), a violent young ranch hand who continuously quarrels with Bick while dreaming of the day he will make his own million. He is convinced that his new property is the beginning of his fortune and his dreams will soon come true. He strikes oil and goes on to great riches. Leslie and Bick have three children who, when grown up, all go against the wishes of their parents. Their son, Jordy, announces his marriage to Juana, a beautiful Mexican girl who is studying medicine. Bick is dismayed at the idea of having a Mexican girl as Mrs. Jordan Benedict III. Reluctantly, all the Benedicts accept an invitation to the elaborate opening of the new hotel owned by the now fabulously wealthy Jett Rink. Bick is furious to discover his daughter Luz as Queen of Jett's spectacular model parade. When Juana is refused service in the beauty salon of the hotel, an enraged Jordy looks for Jett, whom he considers responsible for the insult to his wife. He finds him in the banquet room as Jett is about to deliver his dedication speech. Before Jordy can land a punch, two henchmen pin his arms back while Jett knocks him out. Bick then challenges Jett to a fight outside, but Jett is so drunk and helpless that Bick leaves him in disgust. Later, Jett passes out cold on the speaker's dais before he can deliver his speech. Young Luz is angry at Jordy and for the way she thinks they have disgraced the family and ruined Jett's big evening and goes to the darkened banquet room where the still drunk Jett is delivering his speech to an empty room. Completely disillusioned, Luz returns to her parents. Bick and his family drive to Reata. In a mood of relief and good cheer, they stop by a diner on the highway. A burly young man eyes Luz with distaste, and shortly afterwards orders some impoverished Mexican travellers out. Bick fights him but is no match for the much younger man and ends up on the floor. Back at Reata, Bick grumbles to Leslie that he has been a failure, that nothing has worked out as he planned it. In Leslie's eyes, Bick was at last fighting for fundamental justice and she yells at him: 'After a hundred years, the Benedict family is a real big success.'

In *East of Eden*, as an unknown doing his first starring role, Jimmy had gotten a great deal of personal attention from the director. In *Rebel Without a Cause*, he was not only the star, he had also taken a hand in the writing and directing. In *Giant*, his part would be much smaller than that he had played in either previous movie, and he would be working with well-established stars and under a director who had made his first film in 1924, seven years before Jimmy was born. He went from tadpole in big puddle to big frog in small puddle to not-so-big frog in big puddle.

Jimmy first heard about *Giant* while he was working on

East of Eden. Soon afterward, he discovered that George Stevens and Fred Guiol were working on the script in an office near his dressing room. Whenever he had a few minutes free, he would walk over and hang out. He put to use all the shoot-the-breeze-with-receptionists-flirt-with-secretaries skills he had acquired making the rounds in New York and soon managed to break through to Stevens himself. They chatted about horses, about cars, about photography, and, every so often, Jimmy would say: "Hey, Mr. Stevens, that part of Jett Rink in *Giant* —that's for me." But Stevens had another set of looks in mind for Jett Rink. "Jimmy," says Stevens, "seemed far from the character that we had in mind—a kind of a rigger—and given Jimmy's personality, his size and his style, the role was a tremendous burden for him, but he was quite an able chap." Stevens was also worried about Jimmy's capacity to age convincingly, an important requirement of the screenplay's later scenes. Jett Rink, as the script defines him, is: "A poor boy who makes a hundred million dollars. Tough, always angry, restless, bewildered and reckless, with animal charm and a tycoon's magnetism. He gets his way and loses his way with equal violence. Clever with his hands. (Age: starts about 21, goes through 45.)"

But Jimmy kept hanging around and he kept asking, and finally, after Alan Ladd rejected the role, Stevens let him read the script. The next morning, he showed up at the office, ablaze with enthusiasm, and the director allowed as how he might just let him do Jett Rink.

By the time the filming of *Giant* started, the success of

East of Eden had made Jimmy a lot more important to the studio than he had been when he begged George Stevens for a part. Jane Deacy and Dick Clayton were negotiating for a seven-year contract that would pay him $100,000 per film and allow the making of outside pictures as well. One of the loan-out deals kicking around Warner Brothers was a bid MGM had put in for Jimmy to play Rocky Graziano in *Somebody Up There Likes Me*, and Paramount had mentioned the possibility of renting Jimmy for the Jim Piersall role in *Fear Strikes Out*. Another of Warner Brothers' pet projects involved starring Jimmy in a Western which would present Billy the Kid not as a Hi-Ho Silver hero of the "Old West" but as a baby-face, cold-cock killer. There was also executive-dining-room talk of putting Jimmy in the film version of *Damn Yankees*, which the studio had just bought from Broadway. Negotiations on his new contract were still going on when he left for location.

Ten weeks of the *Giant* shooting schedule were spent in southwest Texas near the little town of Marfa. The Mexican border was less than an hour's drive south. Daytime temperatures climbed to 120 degrees in the shade. There was one hotel and two movie houses, both of which showed Mexican films.

It happened that Joe Brown, the young actor who had known Jimmy in Theatre Arts at UCLA, had been cast (under his film name, Victor Millan) in the part of Mexican ranch hand Angel Obregon. He remembers arriving on location early in July: "It was suppertime when we got there. Jimmy came into the dining room and he looked, and I saw him recognize me, and I was introduced to him as Victor Millan, and he said, 'Hi, Joel' And I thought that was kind of nice.

"And Jimmy was very nice, very pleasant, but then all of a sudden he'd change like that. And that night I remember that Jimmy and Bob Hinkle (the cast's Texas talk coach) and Joe DiAngelo (who doubled for Jimmy in long shots) were going to go out in a jeep that had a light on it and hunt jack rabbits and coyotes. And then they came back later and Jimmy teased the girls with the jack rabbits and the coyotes which were all shot to hell. And I went with them once, and Jimmy drove like a madman. He would laugh, like he was purposely trying to scare me.

"And I thought that was sort of strange because I knew Jimmy as a very quiet, sensitive, kind person. But physically, Jimmy had gotten more muscular. He was heavy, heavier. And I noticed what I call the New York Actors Studio slouch, all the mannerisms. When he'd forget, he'd lose the mannerisms and then he'd remember that he had to have the mannerisms, and I noticed the key thing was the change in his speaking pattern. He would Steve McQueen it. Brando did that and then everybody did it.

"But there's one thing that had remained with him from the days at UCLA. Before he'd go on stage, he wouldn't be like some of the other cats who'd be playing around; he'd get quiet and then *go on!* He did the same thing on *Giant.* I'd hang around and watch him shoot and I noticed his concentration, that *tremendous concen-*

tration. I mean, he'd be so absorbed in a scene that a gun could have gone off and he wouldn't have heard it. He'd play around way before he did a scene, but then slowly you'd see this metamorphosis starting to take place. And I think a lot of people misinterpreted that, thinking him kind of snobbish, but an actor has to do that."

One morning, Joe Brown had a late call and he was standing in front of the hotel waiting for the stretch-out (a long airport-style car used to taxi cast and crew to and from the set). Jimmy, who also had a late call, pulled up in one of the luxurious air-conditioned limousines reserved for stars and invited Joe to ride with him.

They were alone in the back of the big car. Jimmy looked out the window. Joe talked a little about their days at UCLA. At one point Jimmy asked: "Is Baiano still at Warners?" "Hell," said Joe, "you ought to know." A moment passed. Then, quietly, clearly, Jimmy said: "That son-of-a-bitch. I wonder what he thinks now?" Joe remembered something that had happened at UCLA. Jimmy had cut classes to go out to Warner Brothers and drop off his picture. Solly Baiano, head of casting, had told him that he would never make it in the movies because he was too short.

The *Giant* location was a ten-acre plot George Stevens had picked because it was covered with white buffalo grass. He wanted bright ground as contrast to the Benedicts' somber Victorian mansion. "Suddenly," says the script, "the large, castle-like, main house of Reata looms enormous on the flat plain."

"They didn't build the inside," says Joe Brown, "they

just built the façade. And I understand it's still drawing people. That Stevens had a great sense of publicity, because he roped off a place where all the people could come and the people were coming from the nearby towns —in fact, even some of the millionaires were flying down there, and he'd wine and dine them. I knew he was selling tickets because whoever came there was going to go out and see that damn mansion. But he did rope them off.

"Stevens was quite a disciplinarian. He ran things like a general. But he was kind with the actors, gentle with the actors. He had a way of getting a thing out of you. And Jimmy was very, I wouldn't say docile, but he was able to be directed by Stevens. Jimmy gave Stevens a lot of respect as a director."

Jane Withers (Vashti Snythe in the film) also played a role in Jimmy's life on location. Stevens had rented a house for her in Marfa which came to be known as Withers' USO. From Los Angeles, she had brought records, books, games, and goodies to keep the cast and crew entertained. From experience in making more than a hundred movies, she knew that everybody was going to get bored out of his or her brains in a tiny, sun-broiled Texas town. Withers' USO had one rule: Canasta, cold cuts, and Canada Dry okay, booze and poker taboo. "Folks," she says, "have to be occupied with good thought."

At first Jimmy didn't show up very often. When Jane ran into him at lunch or at the location, she would say: "Why in the world don't you come over and get to know people?" As the weeks passed, he began to appear more often. He would sit across the street in the little Chevrolet convertible the studio had rented for him and wait until Jane had rung her special eleven o'clock curfew. When all her other guests had gone, he would "drop in" and talk for an hour or so. Sometimes, behaving more like a pet animal than a pet person, he would climb in through an open window rather than use the door.

Jane, although she was usually tired, and frequently had to get up for a 4 A.M. call next morning, would make an effort to be attentive and sympathetic. She had long since spotted Jimmy as a person engulfed in insecurities. "But," she says, "I try to take every single human being as he or she is. I never judge somebody or wonder why they are the way they are. I thought I could teach Jimmy that everything is not negative and wrong, that he had something to give and didn't always have to try to get."

Eventually, Jimmy and Jane got to know each other really well, and although Jane was only six years older than Jimmy, she came to think of him, and sometimes called him, her "Number 3 son." Often, at their after-the-party sessions, they would read the Bible together—Psalms or certain passages of Matthew which Jane particularly liked. Sometimes they just talked: music, books, psychology, philosophy. One evening, Jimmy told Jane he had been hunting for *War and Peace* and couldn't find it anywhere in her "USO" library or in town.

Later that week, Jane, who had announced a "Monopoly marathon," flew to El Paso to buy up all the sets she could lay hands on. She took time out to find *War and Peace* for Jimmy. "When I gave it to him," she says, "he was so thrilled that he burst into tears and gave me such a hug that I felt we had walked over a great long bridge."

Whenever Jane worked in front of the camera, Jimmy would show up to watch and, since he knew that she had only recently recovered from an attack of rheumatoid arthritis, he would keep asking her if she was okay. To save her strength, he would run errands for her or take her shopping and carry her bags and packages.

One night, he begged her to come along on a rabbit and coyote shoot with him and the Texas talk coach, Bob Hinkle. Reluctantly, she agreed. Hinkle, in an "as told to" piece in a 1956 fan magazine, gives a description of the event which is so glaringly savage and sexist that even a professional Texan might not consider it good personal propaganda today. "One night, I'll admit," says Hinkle, "we were suckers. Jane Withers begged so hard to go along that we took her and another girl with us. You know how girls are. They practically cried every time we shot at a rabbit. That night, we got a coyote—darndest creature. We shot at him four or five times. Each shot knocked him down but didn't kill him. He'd get up and run again. Finally, he couldn't run any more. He lay down by the fence at the side of the road.

"I went up to put him out of his misery, but the girls couldn't stand it. They almost had a fit, screaming and shrieking to let him live. Well, coyotes are real pests in Texas and hated by everyone there and I'm a born Texan. I couldn't be so cruel as to leave that poor animal to suffer, yet it was useless for Jimmy and me to try and explain that to Jane and her friend. Being girls, they were just too tender-hearted for hunting trips. We never took them again." Jimmy's Jett Rink learned a lot more from coach Hinkle than an authentic "Texian" accent.

Whenever he had any time off from the picture, Jimmy liked to take people (like Joe Brown, or anybody else he could talk into the seat beside him) on hair-raising rides. He would jam the accelerator of the dusty little Chevrolet to the floor and roar down the long straight roads as though he thought he could overtake the horizon. Sometimes, he would even run the car across open country, gunning through arroyos, dodging cows and fences, testing his nerve in completely unknown terrain. Finally, George Stevens had a bellyful of the chances Jimmy was taking with a five-million-dollar production. He confiscated the car and ordered Jimmy not to get behind the wheel so he would stay alive to show up in front of the camera.

Jimmy began nagging Jane Withers to let him drive her car, a small Nash she had nicknamed "Little Miserable." She refused. Then, shooting a scene, she sprained her ankle and Jimmy took advantage of her incapacity to insist that he drive. "I just want to feel the car," he kept saying. "I just want to feel the car." She told him that she was taking a big risk letting him drive, considering her dedication to the picture and her friendship with George Stevens, but Jimmy begged so hard that she gave in.

In a few seconds, he had pushed "Little Miserable" up to seventy. Jane began shouting, "Let me out of this car! Jimmy! Stop this car and let me out!" Jimmy stopped.

Jane got out and started to limp toward town. Jimmy drove "Little Miserable" alongside her at snail speed.

"Please, get back in," he pleaded. "Please, Jane. Please."

"My foot hurts," she said, continuing to walk, "but my feelings hurt more. You've let me down. I'm disappointed. I want to trust you. I love you and I love them (the other members of the cast and crew), so I don't drive seventy miles an hour."

"Please, get back in," Jimmy said, over and over. He was on the edge of tears.

Jane kept walking. Jimmy kept creeping along beside her in "Little Miserable." Jane remembers thinking that Jimmy had turned into "Little Miserable" at that moment.

"If you could just trust yourself," she said, after another fifty feet. "If you could just trust yourself, your whole life could change."

"Please, get back in," Jimmy said. "Please get back in. I wouldn't hurt you for anything in the world. I really wouldn't."

Silence.

But after a few more steps, Jane got back into the car. Jimmy drove to town, slowly, safely. He never again tried to frighten her.

George Stevens describes the relationship that existed between him and Jimmy as a "rapport of challenge." This director's ability to "work with actors" is attested to by a film record that includes *Woman of the Year* (Spencer Tracy, Katharine Hepburn), *The Talk of the Town* (Cary Grant, Jean Arthur, Ronald Colman), *A Place in the Sun* (Montgomery Clift, Elizabeth Taylor, Shelley Winters),

Shane (Alan Ladd, Jean Arthur, Van Heflin, Brandon de Wilde). There is no lack of temperament on that list.

While he was working on the script for *Giant,* Stevens saw *East of Eden* and thought Jimmy's role as Cal Trask "a touching part." He also saw *Rebel Without a Cause,* which he describes as having been done "for the matinee crowd and not serving anybody at all well."

He respected Jimmy's ability, but not without certain reservations: "It was quite an imposition on Jimmy's acting talent to play a mumbling, sodden, drunken old man whose dialogue reveals his attraction for Bick's wife."

JETT
(Tears flow, without sadness
from his alcoholic eyes)

Poor boy Jett . . . fighting for what's good . . .
poor Jett . . . flunky for the great Benedicts.
Pretty Leslie. Grand Mrs. Bick . . . poor boy
. . . pretty Leslie . . . June girl bride . . . poor
boy . . . beautiful . . . woman a man wants . . . a
man's got to have. Yeah . . . old proud
king Bick . . . king cow farmer . . .'s got
the do-re-mi . . . Jett boy . . . Benedict's
got it . . . you get it . . . Benedict's got
what he wants . . . the buzzard!

Stevens continues: "That was a rough chore, playing it as he did in his quiet fashion. There was a danger with Jimmy. He would often fragment his work, stretch the stasis until it almost risked not being understood by the

James Dean

audience. Nevertheless, his work in that scene was brilliant and his playing was an invention in itself."

Some people, who are still at Warner Brothers, and who do not want to be named, remember that while Stevens was editing *Giant*, he did, in fact, become so dissatisfied with Jimmy's disjointed reading of Jett Rink's already disjointed last speech that he brought Nick Adams in to dub it for the final cut.

But most of Jimmy's work stayed in the film; and Stevens remembers that on at least one occasion, he regretted not having taken Jimmy's advice. "In the scene in which Jett takes a nip from a bottle at the little bar before he goes into the big party, Jimmy suggested that he (Jett Rink) take a nip from his own flask. I turned him down because I was always having to rope him in, but I now realize that he was right and that such a gesture would have been a more subtle indication of Jett Rink's character." It would have underlined the fact that Jett, now rich and powerful and surrounded by friends, subordinates and servants, was still the defiant "loner" he had been as a poor cowhand on the Benedict ranch.

When the company came back from Texas to do the interior sequences on the Warner lot, Stevens, because he was no longer handling armies of extras, not to mention herds of cattle, had a better chance to observe Jimmy as an individual. "He wanted," Stevens says, "to do all things well, even to spitting a cherry pit further than the next fellow—but he bowed to that fellow if to him belonged the victory. Once, on a set, he did an imitation of Charlie Chaplin and afterward, a friend of his, Nick

Adams, did an imitation of Marlon Brando. Jimmy roared at Nick's, waved aside his own Chaplin takeoff and begged Nick to repeat his." How keenly Nick Adams (who committed suicide by taking an overdose of paraldehyde in 1968) must have felt the irony of being called in later to do an imitation of Jimmy doing Jett Rink!

"I used to feel," says Stevens, "that he was a disturbed boy tremendously dedicated to some intangible beacon of his own and neither he nor anyone else might know what it was. I used to feel this because at times, when he fell quiet and thoughtful as if innerbidden to dream about something, an odd and unconscious sweetness would light up his countenance. At such times, and because I knew he had been motherless since early childhood and had missed a lot of the love that makes boyhood jell right, I would come to believe that he was still waiting for some lost tenderness."

THIRTEEN

Jimmy was glad to get back to Hollywood after the long, hot weeks on location in Texas; and one of the people he was happiest to see again was Pasquale "Patsy" D'Amore, owner of the Villa Capri, an excellent restaurant which has godfathered the best Italian places in Beverly Hills. The people who started La Scala, Stefanino's, Matteo's, Puccini, Martone Marquis, all worked first for Patsy D'Amore.

Patsy grew to feel that Jimmy was "like my own boy." Jimmy felt so much at home with Patsy that he would eat dinner at the Villa Capri night after night. After parking his Triumph motorcycle or his Ford station wagon or his Lancia scooter or his Porsche Speedster out in back, he would come in through the kitchen door. If there were no free tables in the dining room, he would eat at a little table in the pantry usually reserved for the chef.

The Villa Capri was small, but it catered to some of Hollywood's biggest stars, and especially to the so-called Homsby Hills Rat Pack, of which Frank Sinatra, Humphrey Bogart, Lauren Bacall, Sid Luft, and Judy Garland were charter members. But the Capri was not a Brando hangout. Brando came in once and asked for a table. When Patsy told him politely: "Mr. Brando, it will be a few minutes," the star shrugged, muttered something Patsy took to be, "I don't wait," and stalked out into the night never to darken (or brighten) the Capri's door again. Patsy is passionately partisan on the subject of Dean versus Brando. "You can't compare Jimmy with Marlon Brando. Marlon Brando, to me, is nothing. He's an idiot. But Jimmy, well, the personality was him, really natural."

Jimmy never became "big buddies" with any members of the Rat Pack, but he was nevertheless treated with respect—the slightly grudging, slightly sarcastic respect that his accelerating star power elicited from that competitive clique.

Bogart teased Jimmy about his sloppy clothes (movie people of that era put on jacket and tie to go out for dinner), but Sinatra did not forget to invite him to a party he gave at the Villa Capri to send Patsy off on a trip to Naples. That was the only occasion on which Patsy can remember seeing Jimmy wear a tie.

The restaurant was closed to the public and, since Patsy, who did the cooking himself in those days, was flying out the very next morning, the kitchen was closed, too. Sinatra had ordered Mexican food sent in. "At that time," Patsy says, "Mexican food was the worst junk. Not like it is today." But the bar was open and the drinks were first-rate and quite a few people got loaded.

Not Jimmy. Patsy never saw him drunk. All evening long, he would sip a scotch and water and chain smoke king-size Chesterfields. Sometimes, he would play a little game. Instead of using an ashtray, he would set his cigarette down so that it balanced on the butt end. From time to time, he would pick it up, take a puff and, then, careful not to disturb the ash, set it down again. When the ash looked as though it would certainly topple, he would pincer the butt between thumb and forefinger, lift it gingerly, and see if he could make it to the nearest wastebasket or fireplace. People would be either amused or irritated by this perilous little parlor trick, but Jimmy didn't really care which. He could only feel comfortable when he was hidden behind a screen of stunts.

Shortly after he came back from Texas, Jimmy moved out of the Sunset Plaza Drive apartment into an odd little studio house in Sherman Oaks, a suburban part of Los Angeles in the San Fernando Valley. According to Patsy D'Amore, the place appealed to Jimmy because it was "screwy! There was a balcony with a bed, and from there you could see a big floor with a fireplace and the kitchen right in the back."

Jimmy had found the perfect bachelor quarters. For the first time in his life, he put some real effort into fixing up a place to live. From the rafters, he hung two gigantic speakers to satisfy his need for music at ear-shattering volume. In one corner, he set up his two tape machines, a V-M and an Ekotape. He liked to record conversations and improvisations. In another corner, on its tripod, he displayed his 8mm zoom lens Bolex movie camera. He planned one day to shoot a film and often practiced on people who came to the house. There was also an easel on which he would show off a painting or a drawing in progress. At one point, he worked for weeks on a huge pencil sketch of himself lying in a coffin.

One of the women Jimmy saw most frequently during this period was a young actress under contract to Universal-International. Jimmy's agent, Dick Clayton, arranged the first date. According to Maila Nurmi, who was Jimmy's friend but not his lover, Jimmy's affair with this young woman was "on for a long while, but he had no respect for her. He was ashamed of his relationship with her. He felt he was using her—for physical reasons. She was the voluptuous pin-up lady. He used to see her, I guess, almost every evening and we'd (Jack Simmons and Maila) see him later. And if he had to make a public appearance, he made it with her, and he also made private appearances with her, but he was ashamed of it. To us, he didn't even want to talk about it. But Ursula Andress he loved."

Again, it was Dick Clayton who played Cupid. One afternoon, he took Jimmy over to Ursula's apartment. "Dean," she says, "walked in and started searching the house. He stalked all through it, then came in, sat down on the sofa and started staring at me, saying nothing."

After a long silence, Ursula asked Jimmy why he was being so quiet. He began to talk and kept on talking for hours.

Later, he invited Ursula to dinner. After dinner, they dropped in at a club with a Calypso group. But only a few moments after they had been seated, Jimmy excused himself and was gone for what seemed to Ursula an extraordinarily long time.

Then she noticed that he was on the club stage, banging a bongo drum with the band. She could see that she was being ignored. She walked out, hailed a cab, and went home.

An hour later, Jimmy showed up on his motorcycle. He apologized. She forgave him. Then, he talked her into getting onto the back of the motorcycle and they were off on the breakneck initiation ride he so frequently imposed on new friends.

In the weeks their relationship lasted, Ursula would often spend nights and days at a time in Jimmy's Sherman Oaks house, but she never gave up her own bachelor quarters. She had grown up in World War II Europe and was far more mature than the average American girl of her age. Unlike Pier Angeli, she had not been an overprotected child.

Paramount had signed her and planned to put her in a movie as soon as she learned enough English. "I was bewildered in America and even more confused when I came to Hollywood," she says. "I could not speak your language and there was so much of America that I could not understand. Everyone was trying to be nice, but no one was helpful. Then I met Jimmy. You know what was the first thing we did? We got into an argument about American music. Only then did I feel American."

As the affair continued, the arguments got more and more frequent, more and more public, and shifted from sweet, seductive abstraction to acrid personal accusation. Finally, exhausted by Jimmy's unpredictable ups and his more predictable downs, Ursula ditched him for actor John Derek, who was five years older than Jimmy and a lot more experienced (with both war service and a broken marriage to prove it).

Jimmy "torched" (as Maila Nurmi puts it) after Ursula for weeks. He followed her about on his motorcycle. He telephoned her at odd hours of the night. He confronted her and Derek in restaurants. Once, he even stared at them through the window of their parked car. But it didn't work. Nothing worked. Ursula had had it!

It had been possible to lay at least part of the blame for Pier Angeli's rejection of him on her domineering mother. But this was different. Ursula had obviously done her own rejecting. "Jimmy just couldn't believe that anybody could leave him for another man," says Maila Nurmi. "He was stunned."

He found some relief in his friendship with Sanford and Beulah Roth. *Collier's* magazine had asked Roth, an important photographer (whose work included photo essays on Einstein, Picasso, Chagall, Colette, Cocteau) to shoot a story on James Dean, the bright new star of *Giant.*

When Roth introduced himself to Jimmy on the set, Jimmy recognized him as the photographer who had done one of his favorite books on Paris. "That book," said Jimmy, "makes me realize I've never been anywhere. I want to be in Paris before this year is out. I want to see the Paris theatre—to see Pierre Blanchard and Gérard

Philipe. I want to see the great artists—to see Rome—to buy shoes and crazy clothes in Capri. I want to live."

Later that same day, Jimmy asked Roth if he happened to have any of the work of the famous artists he had photographed. When Roth said that many of them had given him paintings and drawings, Jimmy burst out: "When can I come and see you?"

Roth invited Jimmy for dinner that very night and Jimmy kept him and his wife up until five in the morning, talking, talking, talking. But the Roths got to like him and when they found out that he had done some drawing and sculpture himself, and that he wanted to go on studying, they introduced him to artist Pegot Waring. "In the beginning," she says, "it appeared that Jimmy wanted to learn the fine points of sculpture. I was his teacher for that; but I soon learned that he possessed the most insatiable thirst for knowledge of any young man I've ever known. After his second or third lesson, he wanted to hear me explain the technique sculptors use to carve faces in mountains such as Rushmore. His quest for artistic truth was frightening. He wanted to know just about every single fact, idea, theory that had been discovered by man clear back to the stone age. He was much too suspicious of people, but he had a tremendous respect for any who had knowledge."

Sanford Roth and Pegot Waring weren't the only people who understood Jimmy's lonely search for affection. Once, during a party at the Roths', Elizabeth Taylor noticed how fond Jimmy was of their Siamese cat, Louis, who, it was said, had once stalked across Picasso's palette and then been honored by having his paws cleaned by the great man himself. Several days later, Elizabeth called Jimmy over to her dressing room on the *Giant* set and surprised him with a Siamese kitten. Jimmy named him Marcus after his uncle in Indiana.

During his lunch break, Jimmy would often zip home from Warner Brothers to feed the kitten. Before he went out in the evening, he would make sure that Marcus had plenty of food, water, and a clean pan. Many nights, too, he would come home earlier than had been his habit because he did not want Marcus to get lonely. He loved to play with the kitten and watch the kitten play. He tied some twine into a knot and suspended it from a beam. Marcus would bat the knot, purring and growling, sometimes sinking his claws into it so deeply that he would be lifted off the floor and swung back and forth, a pussycat pendulum.

Elizabeth Taylor had come to like Jimmy in spite of some difficult early encounters. He had been very nice at their first meeting, very nasty at their second. But her co-star, Rock Hudson, never changed his feelings. "I didn't like him particularly," says Hudson. "He and I and Chill Wills lived in a rented house together for three months while we were doing *Giant* in Texas and, although we each went more or less our own way, Dean was hard to be around. He hated George Stevens, didn't think he was a good director, and he was always angry and full of contempt. He never smiled. He was sulky and he had no manners. I'm not that concerned with manners—I take them where I find them—but Dean didn't have 'em. And he was rough to do a scene with for reasons that only an actor can appreciate. While doing a scene, in the giving and taking, he was just a taker. He would suck everything out and never give back."

The most serious confrontations between Dean and Stevens were not about interpretation or script. They were about schedule. Getting up at the break of day, reporting to the studio for several hours of costume and make-up and then getting out on the set at eight o'clock sharp only to find that you are not used until late morning or even late afternoon is a hurry-up-and-wait ordeal that actors usually handle with cards (Omar Sharif once said he was a better bridge player than an actor), books, magazines, newspapers, cigarettes, coffee, and gossip. But Jimmy was too intense a person and too intent on his role to weather the waiting that way.

Games and gossip destroyed the deep concentration he needed to do his best in front of the camera. Unlike most of the long-time movie pros he was working with, he could not simply walk out of a coffee klatsch and into the life of a scene. After trying it the studio way for several weeks, he decided to work out his own early-warning system. He asked an assistant director to call him at home shortly before any of his scenes came up, allowing, of course, enough time to drive to the studio and get into make-up and costume.

For a while, the system worked. But one Saturday morning, when a Mercedes McCambridge scene was scheduled, Jimmy decided it would be safe to leave the phone in its own company for a few hours while he picked up some things for the house. Five minutes after he drove off, the phone started to ring and did not stop. Mercedes McCambridge had fallen in the shower and cut her face. One of Jimmy's scenes was up instead.

Assistant directors spent the whole morning calling around town to find him. The production came to a dead stop. George Stevens' anger boiled over into rage. On a hunch, Elizabeth Taylor jumped into her car and drove over to the Sherman Oaks house. Jimmy had just come home when she arrived. She drove him back to the studio. Stevens dressed him down in front of the entire company. Hollywood, said the infuriated director, could do without Jimmy's kind. It would, in fact, be a tremendous relief if Jimmy would go back to his beloved New York and stay there forever. When Stevens stopped shouting, work began again.

During the last weeks of the *Giant* shooting schedule, a young actor, who had known Jimmy in New York, came out to Los Angeles to work in a television series. "I used to see him," the actor remembers, "and one of the spectacular things about him was that he always looked so different (in real life) than he looked on screen. Like, I couldn't have been more astonished when I saw *East of Eden* and this magic creature appeared, because he didn't look like that. I just never saw him look like that. He was never pulled together. He was generally quite filthy—I mean, really filthy: heavy dandruff and the whole scene. But really bad. He looked, I'd say, older than thirty.

"And when he was making *Giant*—in the morning lots

of people would be working, you'd have a six-thirty call, and you'd go down to this place called Huff's. It was just a couple of tables and a counter. And I used to eat there and Jimmy used to eat there, so I would see him from time to time. And one morning, I looked up and he really looked particularly bad, I mean, really bad. And I thought, My God, I mean, what can it be? Then maybe we were both in there a week later and he looked even worse. And I wondered, God, how can he be shooting a movie looking like that? And I realized that he must be aging in *Giant* and that instead of doing pieces (hairpieces), they were shaving his hairline, aging him, giving him that receding hairline, and they were obviously shooting the scenes in continuity so that he looked older and older and with the quality of his face, which always looked older anyway, he really did look like an aging man."

FOURTEEN

By the third week of September 1955, Jimmy's work on *Giant* was complete and he had a few days to himself before rehearsals began for his next assignment, the role of poor boy Morgan Evans in an NBC-TV production of Emlyn Williams' play, *The Corn Is Green.*

Even in his best live television days, Jimmy's price had never climbed out of the hundreds. But now, after *Eden*'s success, and with the promise of *Rebel* and *Giant,* Jane Deacy could ask twenty thousand for a single TV appearance and get it. So the NBC contract was definite and the MGM loan-out (*Somebody Up There Likes Me,* at the new $100,000 a picture price) was almost a sure thing and another pressure was added to those already cooking Jimmy's brain: more money than he knew how to handle.

To help Jimmy hang onto some of his earnings (no easy thing in easy-come-easy-go Hollywood), Jane Deacy and Dick Clayton found him a pair of professional business managers, Carl Coultee and William Gray. They would show the young star how to put his money into the market, into real estate, into burgeoning businesses, and one day he might be as rich as Bob Hope or Bing Crosby or Frank Sinatra. But even before he began to benefit from his new managers' advice, Jimmy had determined to make two important investments.

One was a $100,000 Lloyds of London policy on his life. Lew Bracker, a young insurance agent, made the arrangements. Composer Lenny Rosenman, Lew's cousin, first brought Jimmy to the pleasant Hollywood house-around-a-pool where Lew lived with his parents. The Brackers also owned a ranch, El Capitan, in Santa Barbara, where Jimmy boarded the Palomino stallion (Cisco) he had bought after Kazan warned him off car and motorcycle capers during the shooting of *Eden*.

But knowing that between pictures the studio couldn't put so much pressure on him not to drive, and having learned that horseback riding, much as he loved Cisco, did not ease his itch for speed, he decided to make a high-power racing car his second important investment.

From Competition Motors (a small company that later boomed into Volkswagen Pacific), Jimmy bought a $6,900 Porsche Spyder, quite a spurt ahead both in performance and price from his first Porsche, a $3,700 Speedster. This purchase put Jimmy into an automotive elite whose membership was even more restricted in 1955 than it is today. After World War II, Dr. Porsche and his son, "Ferry," struggled back into production at Stuttgart, but by 1955 the factory was still producing only two or three hundred cars a year.

In any case, Jimmy was less interested in being part of an exclusive set than he was in owning and driving a magnificent machine. The company he preferred was not that of fellow Porsche owners, but that of the mechanics at the Competition Motors garage: Horst Rieschel, Tony Buechler, and Rolf Wuetherich. Working along with these men, he felt at home again. It was like being back with the boys at Marvin Carter's motorcycle shop in Indiana.

Jimmy became friends with twenty-eight-year-old Rolf Wuetherich, the youngest of the three mechanics. Their acquaintance began at road racing circuits (Bakersfield, Santa Barbara, La Jolla) where Jimmy drove his first Porsche, the Speedster, and Rolf serviced factory cars. It was Rolf who told Jimmy, one September afternoon, when he ran into him on Hollywood Boulevard, that the garage had just gotten in a Spyder.

The next day, Jimmy dropped in at Competition Motors, drove the Spyder once around the block, and returned to say he would take it on condition that Rolf personally prepare the car for every race and accompany it as mechanic at every race. Rolf agreed. Jimmy wrote a check.

He was terribly proud of his new racing machine. "After Jimmy finished shooting," says George Stevens, "I was still working with Elizabeth and Rock on the scene they do on the couch at the end. Jimmy came onto the set through the little door and kind of touched me on the shoulder and did some pantomime to let me know that he wanted me to come outside with him. So after a little bit of that, I told the assistant director to save it and went outside with Jimmy through the little door.

"There in the studio street was his little silver Porsche Spyder which sort of looked like a turtle with a cockpit cut into it. So I got in and sat to see how it felt and Jimmy got in beside me and drove me around the lot. And it showed how adroit he was, because when we came back to the sound stage, he dropped me at the big door which the assistant director had now opened to let in some light and air; and everybody, Rock, Elizabeth and the whole crew, came out to see Jimmy in his new car. And he was the center of attention until the studio police came up and told him that they were never going to allow him to bring the automobile onto the lot again, because this was the second time they had caught him doing this and they were going to make sure he didn't interrupt shooting again."

In the last week of September, Jimmy began calling around Hollywood to see if anyone wanted to accompany him to a road race that was scheduled for the weekend of October 1, in Salinas, a town in the heart of *East of Eden* country, about three hundred miles up the coast from Los Angeles.

Jane Withers told Jimmy she just couldn't be away from her kids for a whole weekend. Remembering the incident in Texas with her car, "Little Miserable," she made him promise that he would drive carefully. He promised, but didn't seem at all concerned. It was a lot less dangerous, he told her, to compete in a race with trained drivers than it was to share the highway with the average motorist.

Next he called actor Steve Rowland and suggested going up to Salinas on Thursday so there would be time to put mileage on the Porsche and get the feel of the circuit. Steve said he thought he could go, but telephoned later to say he had an audition.

Then Jimmy called movie bit player Bill Hickman who said he was sure he could make it.

Jimmy also asked Sanford Roth. The photographer said he was too busy editing *Giant* pictures for the forthcoming *Collier's* story. Later that day, however, he called his editors in New York and told them he thought a picture of Jimmy driving in a race would make a great finale for his photo essay. They agreed. He phoned Jimmy back to say he would be going after all.

Jimmy also invited Uncle Marcus Winslow, Uncle Charlie Nolan, and his father to the race at Salinas. The Winslows, it happened, were in Los Angeles, visiting Winton and Ethel Dean; but they wanted to get started back to Indiana. It was a four- or five-day drive and they had been away from the farm long enough. Charlie Nolan Dean and his wife, Mildred, had also come out from Indiana for the family get-together, but they, too, intended to start back by the weekend. Jimmy's father had, as usual, a heavy work load at the dental clinic and could not get away.

Jane Deacy was in town that week, too. She had flown out from New York to complete negotiations on Jimmy's new Warner contract. Jimmy sent flowers to her suite at the Chateau Marmont (Hollywood's funkiest old show business hotel), and drove out to the airport to pick her up. The next evening, she gave a small party in her rooms to celebrate Jimmy's success, which was very much her success, too. She had worked hard, perhaps even harder than Jimmy, for, in addition to her career as an agent, she made a home for her husband, a New York radio engineer, and a teen-age son.

Jimmy seemed to be in an excellent mood at the party. He and Jane talked about the future. They made a plan to fly back to New York together at the beginning of the next week when Jimmy was due at rehearsals of *The Corn Is Green*. They discussed trying to wedge a provision in the new contract which would allow Jimmy to do a play now and then. There were two shows coming up on Broadway which Jane thought might be right for him.

The next evening, Wednesday, Jimmy went to the movies with insurance man Lew Bracker. He told Lew his tentative plan for distribution of the policy's principal sum. He wanted $5,000 to go to Grandma and Grandpa Dean; $10,000 to go to his young cousin Markie Jr. for education; and the balance, $85,000, to go to Marcus and Ortense Winslow. But Lew, feeling that the stipulations of a will would be stronger than those of an insurance policy, especially if the next of kin, in this case Jimmy's father, were not named, advised Jimmy to make his estate the beneficiary of the policy. That way, he could lump the $100,000 with his other assets and let the provisions of the will make the distributions he intended. Jimmy agreed to see a lawyer and draw up a will before he left for New York.

On Thursday afternoon, Jimmy stopped off at the apartment of Jeanette Mille, one of the women he had begun to date after Ursula Andress threw him over. Jeanette was not expecting him. When she came to the door, he pressed his beloved Siamese, Marcus, into her arms, told her the cat was a present, and drove off without another word.

On Thursday night, Jimmy, as he often did before a race, deserted his regular friends and went off by himself. According to a member of a New York S & M club, who was then living in Hollywood, Jimmy went that night to a gay party at Malibu Colony and got involved in a terrible screaming scene. Toward dawn, one of Jimmy's lovers put him "up against the wall" about his sexual identity and demanded that he "come out" once and for all and stop pretending to be sexually interested in women, except, as his accuser put it scornfully, "for publicity purposes."

By eight next morning, September 30, Jimmy was at Competition Motors, peering over Rolf Wuetherich's shoulder as he checked out the Porsche—oil pressure, ignition, spark plugs, tires. Jimmy was impatient. Every so often he would ask Rolf if he needed help and the mechanic would say: "No thanks, you'll only complicate things."

When the check was finished, Rolf installed a safety belt on the driver's seat. He did not put one on the passenger seat because Jimmy would be driving alone in the race.

A few minutes before ten, Jimmy's father and Uncle Charlie Nolan showed up to see Jimmy off. Charlie Nolan had taken Jimmy on his first motorcycle ride and now Jimmy took Charlie Nolan on his first Porsche ride. When they got back to the garage, Charlie Nolan put his arm around Jimmy's shoulder and said, only half in jest, "Be careful, Jim. You're sitting on a bomb!"

After an early lunch, Jimmy and Rolf loaded the Porsche onto the trailer attached to Jimmy's station wagon, said good-bye to Winton and Charlie Nolan and drove out through Laurel Canyon to pick up Sanford Roth and Bill Hickman. At Roth's house, Jimmy decided to take the racer off its trailer and drive it to Salinas so that he and the car could do as much pre-race mileage together as possible. He asked Rolf to ride with him to make sure the engine was in perfect tune.

Jimmy was wearing his usual outfit: light blue pants, white T-shirt, red nylon jacket. Before he got into the Porsche he took the jacket off and threw it behind the seat. Then he snapped dark lenses over his regular glasses and started the engine. He and Rolf, with Sanford Roth and Bill Hickman following in the station wagon, drove out Ventura Boulevard. They stopped for gas, and then headed north on Highway 99.

It was a blue sky day with lots of warm sun. Every once in a while the station wagon would roar past the Porsche. Jimmy would let Roth and Hickman stay ahead for a few miles and then slide past them into the lead again. Rolf was pleased with the engine. It was ticking like a watch. Jimmy, off on his first all-play-no-work adventure in months, was whistling, singing, telling jokes, smoking cigarette after cigarette. From time to time he would elbow Rolf in the ribs and ask, "What's the rev number?" or "How's the oil temp?" or "You sure this is the right road?"

Just before three, he pulled off at a roadside stand and ordered a glass of milk. Rolf didn't want anything, but Jimmy insisted that he drink an ice cream soda. Sucking reluctantly on the soda, Rolf began to think about the next day's competition. It suddenly hit him that Jimmy, who was still far from a seasoned driver, was going to race a car in which he had almost no road time. He looked Jimmy hard in the eyes. "Don't drive fast tomorrow," he said, without smiling. "Don't try to win. The Spyder is something quite different from the Speedster. Don't drive to win. Drive to get experience."

"Okay, okay," Jimmy said, with a grin.

Rolf did not grin back.

"Give me signs when I go round," Jimmy said after a moment, proving that he had heard Rolf after all.

There was another awkward silence. Jimmy pulled a ring from his finger, a tinny souvenir he had picked up in a five and dime. He handed it to Rolf.

"Why?" asked Rolf.

"I want to give you something," Jimmy said, "to show we're friends."

Rolf's hands were much bigger than Jimmy's. The ring would only fit his little finger.

Roth and Hickman pulled up in the station wagon. It had taken them five minutes to catch up.

"Don't let him drive too fast," Roth yelled to Rolf when the two cars set off again.

A little while later, the caravan, Porsche ahead, station wagon and trailer hanging on behind, was speeding down Grapevine Grade, a long, steep incline that brings Route 99 down out of the mountains onto the broad plain just south of Bakersfield.

Officer Otie V. Hunter was cruising up the grade. He spotted a small silver car coming down the hill, moving much too fast. It flashed by, closely followed by a white station wagon towing a light trailer. Hunter did a U-turn through a slot in the median, turned on his siren, and gave chase.

Jimmy made no attempt to outrun the police car. He pulled over and waited for the officer to get out and walk alongside. Politely, Hunter told him he'd been doing 65 in a 45-mile zone. He didn't argue. As Hunter wrote out a ticket, he began to ask Jimmy questions about the Porsche. He'd never seen a car just like it. Soon, the two were chatting like members of the same racing team. Then Hunter handed Jimmy his ticket and walked back to the station wagon and gave Roth one too.

Before starting off again, Jimmy yelled back to the station wagon: "We'll wait for you at Paso Robles. We'll have dinner there."

North of Bakersfield, Jimmy and Rolf turned left onto Route 466 (now Route 46), a narrow, two-way paved road that would take them west to Paso Robles where they would again turn north for Salinas.

"The road was one gray line," Rolf remembers, "cutting through monotonous landscape—here and there a very light bend, otherwise straight ahead. It felt like driving on an endless ruler."

Finally, a low, dark form appeared on the horizon. As they approached, they saw that it was a battered gas-station-restaurant-general store, the only building in Blackwell's Corners, the name given to the intersection of Route 466 and an even less well-maintained north and south road, Route 33.

Jimmy pulled in when he noticed that there was a big, gray Mercedes parked in front of the store. He got out and looked over the car. When its owner, who turned out to be Lance Reventlow, Barbara Hutton's twenty-one-year-old son, came out, Jimmy started a conversation. Lance was driving up to the race at Salinas, too. The two drivers talked until the station wagon caught up again.

"How do you like the Spyder now?" Roth shouted, as he drove in.

"Great," said Jimmy. "I'm going to treat it good. I'm going to keep this baby a long time."

Then Jimmy bought a bag of apples, bit into one, put the bag behind the seat, and got into the Porsche again. Without fastening his seat belt, he started up and roared back out onto the road.

"Everything okay?" Jimmy shouted over to Rolf, a little while later.

"Everything okay," Rolf yawned, half hypnotized by the drone of the engine, the fatigue of a day that had begun at dawn, and the heat of the late afternoon sun, a reddening yellow ball that hung in the sky ahead, looking as though it might drop onto the earth at any moment.

There was no talking now, only the motor, the road and the sun. Through the haze of his exhaustion, Rolf was aware that the road had begun to rise and fall, swelling gently up and down between breast-round hills covered with brown grass. Now they were heading down a longer slope into a little valley.

Sun in the eyes made it hard to see, but there, way down in the trough of the valley, coming around a long curve and preparing to climb the hill, was a white, no, a white and black speck. It was getting larger now, getting larger fast—Jimmy was doing 85—a big two-tone job, black top, white hood. In a few seconds it would slip by in the eastbound lane.

Suddenly, my God, the black-and-white's wheels had crossed over the line into the westbound lane, their lane. The car was coming down on them.

Jimmy screamed, "That guy's got to stop!"

There was a horrible, crunching crash, the tinkle of glass, and then, silence.

Ten minutes later, Roth and Hickman pulled up in the station wagon. In a ditch to the right, they saw the once sleek, aluminum-skinned Porsche, looking, according to Roth, like a "crumpled pack of cigarettes."

A highway patrolman began asking questions. Then Roth recognized Rolf, lying face down on the ground, a few feet from the wreck. Thrown clear! But where was Jimmy? Jesus! There! In the wreck! Draped sickeningly over the driver's door, his head dangling. Neither boy was moving. And over there was the other car, a big black and white Ford sedan, a fender smashed, the driver's side of the windshield shattered, as though a bowling ball had hit it from inside. And there was the driver, stretched out alongside, bleeding from the forehead. But he was moving. A trooper was talking to him.

Around the long curve from the east came a white Buick ambulance, its siren screaming, its red flashers eye-piercingly bright against the darkening sky. Driver Paul Moreno and his assistant, Collier Davidson, stopped beside the mangled Porsche. First they rolled Rolf onto a stretcher and slid him into the ambulance's upper rack. Then, as carefully as they could, they pulled Jimmy out of the wreck and put him in the lower berth. Although driver Moreno makes no claim to medical knowledge, the experience of countless accidents told him that Jimmy was dead when he lifted him off the Porsche's door.

Rolf regained consciousness as the ambulance, roaring along the road toward Paso Robles War Memorial Hospital, swerved violently to avoid an oncoming car. Where is Jimmy? he thought. What happened to Jimmy? Then he saw Jimmy in the lower stretcher, limp, covered with blood, arms and legs sticking out at odd angles, the head in a position that could only indicate a broken neck.

When the ambulance reached the hospital emergency dock, an intern climbed inside, checked Jimmy for vital signs. There were none. Jimmy was officially dead.

Rolf suffered a smashed jaw, a broken leg, multiple contusions, cuts, and abrasions.

The driver of the other car, Donald Gene Turnupseed, a California Polytechnic student, escaped with a bloody forehead and a bruised nose.

FIFTEEN

The news of Jimmy's death hit Hollywood hard.

The operator at the Paso Robles War Memorial Hospital called Warner Brothers and got a studio cop on one of the night lines. The studio cop called the producer of *Giant*, Henry Ginsberg. Ginsberg called Dick Clayton. Clayton called Jane Deacy at the Marmont. The two agents drove to West Los Angeles to tell Winton Dean. They didn't want him to hear the news on the radio, or read it in a newspaper.

Ginsberg also phoned Stewart Stern. "The boy is dead! The boy is dead!" Stern heard Ginsberg saying and knew immediately that his friend meant Jimmy Dean, but could not believe the news. In a daze, he wandered out onto Sunset Boulevard. As he came to Googie's, he noticed that there were knots of people on the sidewalk. Coming closer, he saw that some of the people—mostly young actors and actresses he knew by sight—were crying. Others were staring blankly at passing cars. It was only then that Stern heard himself saying, "My God, it must be true."

George Stevens and several members of the *Giant* cast were screening rushes when "suddenly," Elizabeth Taylor remembers, "the phone rang. I heard him (George Stevens) say, 'No, my God, when? Are you sure?' And he kind of grunted a couple of times and hung up the phone. He stopped the film and turned on the lights, stood up and said to the room, 'I've just been given the news that Jimmy Dean has been killed.' There was an intake of breath. No one said anything. I couldn't believe it, none of us could. So several of us started calling newspapers, hospitals, police, the morgue. The news was not general at that time. After maybe two hours, the word was confirmed. Everybody drifted out to their cars to go home. It was about nine o'clock at night. The studio was deserted. As I walked to my car, feeling numb, I saw a figure coming through the lights down one of the little side streets. It was George, getting into his Mercedes. We looked at each other and I said, 'I can't believe it, George, I can't believe it.' He said, 'I believe it. He had it coming to him. The way he drove, he had it coming.'"

On the day of the accident, Ortense and Marcus Winslow were in the middle of their trip home to Indiana. The next day, Saturday, there had been something about a young movie star's auto accident on the car radio, but Marcus snapped it off before the announcer gave details. When they stopped for the night, he didn't buy a newspaper. The Winslows didn't get the bad news until they got back to Fairmount on Monday.

"There'll never be another boy like him," Ortense told a reporter.

The story was local, national and international news. All the networks, wire services, newspapers, news magazines carried it. The Fairmount *News* put out a special edition under a black-bordered banner head: "IN MEMORY OF JAMES DEAN."

In one of the stories, readers learned that "Winton Dean, father of the young actor, is the only direct heir." Because Jimmy died without a will, his father got all of the $100,000 insurance award and about $5,000 that was left over in his Los Angeles bank account after buying the Porsche. The beneficiaries he had indicated to Lew Bracker—Grandma and Grandpa Dean, Uncle Marcus, Aunt Ortense and their son Markie Jr.—got nothing. In the nine years that the Winslows took care of Jimmy, tho only money they ever received toward his support was the small monthly dependent's check the government sent during Winton's army service.

Another story on page one told Fairmount residents that the accident which had happened in faraway California was going to become an important event in their own quiet Indiana lives: "LAST RITES WILL BE HELD HERE SATURDAY."

A few hours after Winton Dean learned of his son's death, he drove to Paso Robles and made arrangements with Sheriff-Coroner Paul Merrick to have Jimmy's body flown back to Indiana.

On Tuesday evening, October 4, Wilbur Hunt, owner of a funeral service and furniture store in Fairmount, drove his hearse to the Indianapolis airport to meet the plane bringing Jimmy's body home.

On Wednesday, October 5, Winton Dean arrived from California to attend his son's funeral.

Until the burial services, the body remained at the Hunt Funeral Home. This was not the first time Jimmy had occupied one of Mr. Hunt's coffins. On a brief midwinter (February 1955) trip back to Fairmount with photographer Dennis Stock (who had sold a Dean-at-home story to *Life* magazine), Jimmy posed in his uncle's farmhouse, in the barnyard, in the fields, on Main Street, at the high school. Then, one afternoon, he dragged Stock into a furniture store, led him to the back where caskets were displayed, hopped into one, and insisted that Stock shoot a roll of film. On March 7, 1955, *Life* ran "Moody New Star," a four-page picture story on Jimmy. But the casket shot did not appear. The editors had refused to print it.

By ten o'clock on the day of the funeral, Saturday, October 8, special detachments of Indiana State Police had taken up positions at the intersections of the roads leading into Fairmount. Cars were converging on the town from all directions.

By one in the afternoon, all the pews in the Friends Church, except those reserved for Jimmy's family, were occupied. There was no standing room either. When the funeral began at two, the crowd covered the church steps, the lawn, the sidewalk, the street. Three thousand people had come.

Reverend Xen Harvey, pastor of the church, and Dr. James DeWeerd, who was now pastor of Cadle Tabernacle in Indianapolis, conducted the service. Jimmy's old friend DeWeerd, dramatic as usual, had flown in by private plane from Cincinnati, following his regular noontime revival telecast. A state patrol car met him at the Marion airport and sirened him to the church on time.

Dr. DeWeerd based his message to the mourners (heard inside the church only, since the loudspeakers outside failed to work) on James 4:14: "Whereas ye know not what shall be on the morrow. For what is your life? It is even a vapour, that appeareth for a little time and then vanisheth away."

"The only worthwhile things," said the pastor, "are the things that outlast life here. Fame, wealth and pleasure are false goals."

Reverend Xen Harvey's eulogy divided Jimmy's life into "three acts." Act I: Indiana boyhood. Act II: Stardom in Hollywood. And Act III: "James Dean," explained Harvey, "was not brought back to Fairmount. He is not in California, but is enjoying life after death." With theological nicety, the home-town paper announced: "FAIRMOUNT BURIES JAMES DEAN'S BODY."

After the service, six of Jimmy's high school classmates —Paul Smith, Bob Pulley, Bob Middleton, James Fulkerson, Rex Bright, and Whitey Rust—carried the coffin from the church.

The funeral cortege, led by Hunt's big black hearse, moved slowly up Main Street toward Park Cemetery, a long strip of marble-studded green that lies just a few fields south of Marvin Carter's motorcycle shop.

After four days of rain, the sky had cleared. The day was bright, sunny, almost summery, with temperatures in the upper fifties and low sixties. A good part of the crowd followed the hearse to the cemetery.

There, the six pallbearers, assisted by funeral director Hunt, carried Jimmy's body to its grave at the crest of a small hill. A hundred yards away, closer to the road, Jimmy's great-grandfather, Cal Dean, had been buried many years earlier.

Elizabeth Taylor and Edna Ferber sent flowers. Henry Ginsberg and Warner publicity man Steve Brooks came in person. So did Jack Simmons, the faithful friend Jimmy so often met after midnight with Maila Nurmi. Maila couldn't get away from her TV show, but the very next summer, she made a private pilgrimage to the grave. (She traveled by train and, as it neared Indiana, she found herself in the dining car having lunch. When the meal was finished, she felt a strange compulsion to put the shiny metal sugar bowl in her purse. For a long time she fought the urge, but finally succumbed, wondering why she felt an irresistible impulse to steal something for which she had absolutely no need. When she visited the Winslows in Fairmount later that day, she learned that Jimmy had taken the metal sugar bowl from the train which had brought him and his mother's body back from California in 1940. He had wanted something to help him remember that sad last journey.)

Shortly after the burial, a slab of pinkish granite was placed at the head of the grave. On the side facing west, chiseled in roman capitals, is the name JAMES B. DEAN, and below, the birth year, 1931, a long serifed dash, and the death year, 1955. Both name and numbers have been attacked by souvenir hunters. The small triangles inside both "A's" have been broken out. The insides of the "B" are gone. Both "E's," the "M" and the "N" have been scarred. The inside rounds of both "9's" are missing and the top half round of the "3" has been chipped away. Vandalism or veneration? The latter is more likely in a culture which for thousands of years has dragged with it the "relics" of saints and "pieces of the true cross."

Three days after the funeral, on October 11, 1955, a coroner's jury in San Luis Obispo, California, heard testimony about the accident. The first witnesses were Ronald Nelson and Ernie Tripke, the highway patrol officers who had arrived first at the scene. The third witness was Otie V. Hunter, the trooper who gave Jimmy a speeding ticket on Grapevine Grade.

Next came Tom Fredericks, a bookkeeper from Shandon, California, and his brother-in-law, Tom Dooley. They testified that the Porsche had passed them just before it crashed. They said that Wuetherich had on a red T-shirt and that Dean had worn a "white upper garment." They were sure that the man they saw at the wheel just before the collision was wearing red. (Perhaps Jimmy had put his red nylon jacket back on before leaving Blackwell's Corners.)

At Glendale Hospital, where he had been transferred for further treatment, and where he would stay for seven more months, Wuetherich categorically denied this report. He reiterated his earlier statement: he had been Jimmy's passenger for the entire trip. The driver's seat had taken the main impact of the crash. Wuetherich knew perfectly well that if he had been in it he would not have been alive to affirm or deny anything.

Ambulance driver Paul Moreno took the stand next and described how he lifted Jimmy off the driver's door.

Last came the driver of the other car, Donald Gene Turnupseed. He told the jury what he had told the investigating officer: he hadn't seen the other car at all. He had been driving home to Tulare that Friday night to spend a weekend with his parents. When he came around the long slow bend just east of Cholame, the town closest to the accident site, he knew he was going to take the left-hand fork of the Y intersection at the bottom of the little valley. The road splits there: left for Tulare, straight ahead for Bakersfield.

Since there was no boulevard stop at the Y, he had simply slowed down and glanced up the hill to see if any cars were coming from the other direction before starting across the center line into the Y's left fork.

Why hadn't he seen Jimmy? Because Jimmy's car was small, low, and painted a gray, racing silver that served, particularly at that twilight hour—a few minutes before 6 P.M.—to camouflage it rather than make it stand out.

Even if he had seen Jimmy, he might have thought he had time to make it across the road. The Porsche could easily have been mistaken for a normal size car at a much greater distance and, from his dead-ahead perspective, it would have been difficult for him to guess that Jimmy was coming on so fast—thirty miles above the limit. Coroner Merrick pointed out that the Porsche's average speed between the 3:30 P.M. ticket on Grapevine

Grade and the 5:59 P.M. accident on Route 466—allowing for a fifteen minute stop at Blackwell's Corners—had been calculated to be nearly 86 miles per hour.

The jury retired, and in twenty minutes came back with a verdict: Accidental Death. No charges were lodged against Turnupseed.

Had Jimmy lived, he would almost certainly have had to face charges. He was clearly guilty of contributory negligence. No driver could have expected other drivers (or, for that matter, pedestrians, cattle, dogs, or cats) to respond with any margin of safety to a vehicle moving 30 miles per hour above the speed limit.

But in the isolated court of Jimmy's inner law, negligence was probably never a factor. Pushing limits had become a habit for him. He did it every day—emotionally, socially, professionally—with his own physical machine and with all the machines he operated. His last words—"That guy's got to stop"—place the burden of respecting limits on the other person, not on himself.

An individual's sense of limits is absorbed consciously and unconsciously from parents. There is a constant flux of behavioral stimulus and inhibition, and of direct verbal influence: Do this! Don't do that! Most people grow up receiving a fairly well-balanced set of signals. Some people get more of one kind than another. Some people get hopelessly mixed signals. Extremes of any kind are difficult to deal with, but hardest to handle is the absence of any signals at all.

Jimmy lost his mother. Then his father handed him over to an aunt and uncle. Try as they might, these foster parents could not generate signals authentic enough to replace those no longer coming from the real parents.

After only a few years in Indiana, Jimmy knew he could never be a farmer like Uncle Marcus. After only a few months at college, he knew he could never be a lawyer—the role signal his father emitted rather feebly after being off the air for nine years. He could not even take time to be a student actor.

So he left UCLA, found his way to New York, got himself parts in dozens of television shows, two Broadway plays, three Hollywood movies. Every time he pushed reality, it gave: stardom, sex, money. At twenty-four, he had it all—everything except relief from an insatiable craving to fill the emptiness that mocked him with the echo of his own question: Who am I?

Abandonment steers people straight into addiction. It doesn't matter what the addict gets hooked on, there's never enough to fill the ever-widening hole that lost love has opened up in the heart.

At various times in his life Jimmy was hooked on: bongo drums, bullfighting, ballet dancing, rude silence, incessant talk, loud music, drawing, sculpturing, piano playing, recorder tooting, practical jokes, sloppiness, exhaustion, ambition, or any of these in combination with his biggest high: acting.

He was always pushing into new things, pushing into new people, hoping that some thing or somebody would stop him, tell him his limits, tell him who he was. But he kept winning; and nobody tells a winner what to do.

When he got hooked on speed (the Porsche kind, not

the chemical kind), he hoped, as he had with all the other things and people he tried, that it would give him some relief from the ache of abandonment. So he pushed to the limit. The limit turned out to be death.

EPILOGUE

Reverend Xen Harvey had seen Jimmy's life in three parts: Boyhood, Hollywood, and Heaven. But shortly after the funeral, whatever the fate of Jimmy's soul, his image began an afterlife on earth which neither the pastor, nor anyone else, could have foreseen.

There is a feeling in Hollywood that the death of the star before a movie's release may jinx it at the box office. Not knowing what to expect, Warner Brothers opened *Rebel Without a Cause* at the Astor Theatre in New York on October 29, 1955, just three weeks after the funeral.

In addition to the doubts raised by Jimmy's death, the film's release was handicapped by the fact that, in spite of its being in color and Cinemascope, the studio had never really considered it an "A" picture. There was no great investment in advertising, publicity or promotion.

The few, comparatively small ads that did run sold hard on Jimmy (the only "bankable factor"): "The sensation of East of Eden, JAMES DEAN, as a kid from a 'good' family, caught in the undertow of today's juvenile violence." Another said, "This kid has a chip on *both* shoulders. He's Jim Stark, teenager who thinks he has to be bad to make good!" But the studio's basic campaign strategy was simply: "Let's run it up the flagpole and see if anybody salutes."

Someone did. Wanda Hale, in the *Daily News*, awarded *Rebel* three stars, some applause, and a few cat-calls: "The Warner Bros. Cinemascope picture is double grim, horrendous in text, depressing because it is a constant reminder of the tragic death of the star, James Dean. As a starring vehicle for Dean, *Rebel Without a Cause* is satisfactory, giving the late, lamented young actor a role similar to the one he had in his first picture, *East of Eden*. And with complete control of the character, he gives a fine, sensitive performance of an unhappy, lonely teenager, tormented by the knowledge of his emotional instability." But, Miss Hale went on to say: "As an honest, purposeful drama of juvenile hardness and violence, the film just doesn't measure up."

Other reviewers went pretty much the same route. They weren't crazy about the story, but they did feel that Jimmy's acting had enough authority to make the main character work. So Warner Brothers' gamble—releasing the film immediately after Jimmy's death—began to pay off. The picture did well at the Astor, in the "nabes," and across the country.

After the first few unsteady weeks, Warner Brothers began to realize that there was plenty of "life" in their dead star. Through the remaining months of 1955, and for the next three years there was an avalanche of articles and pictures in all levels of print media.

There was plenty of excitement abroad, too. François Truffaut, in the February 1956 *Cahiers du Cinéma*, referred to Jimmy (recalling Baudelaire's *Fleurs du Mal*) as a "freshly cut flower of evil" and gave him an importance in film equal to that of Lillian Gish, Charlie Chaplin, and Ingrid Bergman. Later that same year, in *Arts*, Truffaut said: "In James Dean, today's youth discovers itself. Less for the reasons usually advanced: violence, sadism, hysteria, pessimism, cruelty and filth, than for others, infinitely more simple and commonplace: modesty of feeling, continual fantasy life, moral purity without relation to everyday morality but all the more rigorous, eternal adolescent love of tests and trials, intoxication, pride and regret at feeling oneself 'outside' society, refusal and desire to become integrated and, finally, acceptance or refusal of the world as it is."

The French fan press (magazines like *CinéMonde*, *Cinéma*, *Copains*, *Caline*, *Disco Revue*) was soon engulfed by the Dean media wave and so were similar publications in England, Germany, Italy, Japan, and Israel (where a special Dean bio booklet appeared with Jimmy smiling wistfully amid imposing paragraphs of Hebrew).

But here at home, articles appeared not just by the dozens but by the hundreds. A few titles will describe the character of the mounting Dean obsession. "The End . . . or the Beginning" (*Movie Stars Parade*, May 1956); "Jimmy Dean is Not Dead" (*Motion Picture*, May 1956); "Did Jimmy Dean Really Die?" (*Rave*, May 1956); "Jimmy Dean Still Gets Mail" (New York *World-Telegram and Sun*, May 3, 1956); "The Truth Behind the James Dean Stories," (*Movie Secrets*, June 1956); "Jimmy Dean Fights Back From the Grave" (*Movie Life*, June 1956); "The Boy Who Refused to Die" (*The*

James Dean Album, Ideal, 1956); "Star That Won't Dim" (*Newsweek,* June 18, 1956); "The Strange Revival of James Dean" (*American Weekly,* July 29, 1956); "Macabre Build Up of James Dean" (*Chicago American,* August 10, 1956); "The Legend of James Dean" (New York *Post,* August 19, 1956); "Dean's Still Alive in Death to Fans" (*Florida Times Union,* August 26, 1956); "The Star They'll Never Forget" (*The Real James Dean Story,* Fawcett, 1956); "This Is How the Legend Was Made" (*James Dean Official Anniversary Book,* Dell, 1956); "The Man They Won't Let Die" (*Movie Show,* September 1956); "They Won't Let Him Rest in Peace" (New York *Daily News,* September 29, 1956); "Your James Dean Memorial Medallion" (*Modern Screen,* October 1956); "You Can Make Jimmy Dean Live Forever" (*Motion Picture,* October 1956).

One of the ways thousands of people tried to "make Jimmy Dean live forever" was to purchase one or more of the souvenirs that suddenly appeared everywhere. There were James Dean busts, masks, "wallet pix," jackets, pocket knives, rings (purporting to contain a chip from the gravestone), even slivers of glass, shards of aluminum, and paint scrapings—all supposedly taken from the death car (which turned up later crushed but complete at the December 1956 International Motor Sports Show in Hollywood).

There were LP albums: sound tracks from Jimmy's films, homemade tapes of Jimmy playing the bongo drums, mood music he had once listened to in a Hollywood bar. And there were even more singles: "His Name Was Dean," "The Story of James Dean," "The Racer

Lives Forever," "Jimmy, Jimmy," "The Ballad of James Dean," "Jimmy Dean Is Not Dead," "Hymn for James Dean," "A Boy Named Jimmy Dean."

There were fan clubs, hundreds of fan clubs, in the United States, Canada, Europe, South America and, later, in Japan, Australia and Africa. And the clubs put out mimeographed magazines to further spread the Dean print plague. One such publication, the *James Dean Memorial Club Journal*, brought out an issue entitled, "The Giant." Each copy carried on its blue stock cover a hand-pasted 2¾ by 3¾-inch snapshot of Jimmy (looking very dignified in glasses and tuxedo).

Inside were dedications, drawings, letters ("Dear Jimmy, this letter is meant to say, once and for all, how we feel about you. We love you. Yes, Jimmy, not in a possessive way, but in such a way that we only wanted you to be happy—to lose that inner torment which seemed to be a part of you. And besides this, we loved, and still love, each thing about you. The things we keep in a secret treasury and touch and count as if they were precious jewels—which they are. We love that shock of tawny, uncombed hair. We love your broad forehead and the tiny crease which showed itself between the brows when you were unhappy or perplexed [and we longed to comfort you] . . ."), and there was a section called "News and Views":

GOOD NEWS! . . . We have received word that THE JOSEPH SCHLITZ BREWING COMPANY has decided to re-run the teleplay 'THE UNLIGHTED ROAD' (a drama in which Jimmy played the pawn of truck hi-jackers, and the only live show of his that was recorded on film) on this coming NOVEMBER 16th. Once before, on last June 1st, the play was repeated due to all the requests. The play is presented by THE SCHLITZ PLAYHOUSE OF STARS which appears on Channel 2 at 9:30 P.M. on Friday evenings. We are very grateful to the Joseph Schlitz Brewing Company for once again responding to the many heart-felt requests to re-run Jimmy's performance.

"May we," said the *Journal* on another page, "make a suggestion to any of you who happen to live in the country and have fireplaces in your homes. To save fuel costs, there is a cheap—in more ways than one—product whose only useful purpose is for burning. We speak of the trash publications which dare to print their monstrous lies and distortions about Jimmy. With the photographs of Jimmy cut out, what is left of these symbols of ignorance and depravity is just perfect to be sent up in smoke."

By the time *Giant* opened in New York (October 10, 1956, at the Roxy) the Jimmy Dean boom was as spectacular as Jett Rink's oil strike in the picture.

Bosley Crowther (New York *Times,* October 11, 1956) thought *Giant* "a strong contender for the year's top film award." He had particular praise for Jimmy's performance: "However, it is the late James Dean who makes the malignant role of the surly ranch hand who becomes an oil baron the most tangy and corrosive in the film. Mr. Dean plays this curious villain with a stylized spookiness —a sly sort of off-beat languor and slur of language—that concentrates spites. This is a haunting capstone to the brief career of Mr. Dean."

In the New York *Herald Tribune* on the same morning, Herbert Kupferberg showed some reserve about the film: ". . . perhaps it doesn't dig as deeply as it should into its characters' minds and hearts"; but his praise of Jimmy's performance paralleled Crowther's: ". . . it is James Dean who gives the most striking performance and creates in Jett Rink the most memorable character in *Giant*. Devotees of the cult which has grown up around him since he was killed in an auto crash just after *Giant* was filmed may be somewhat surprised to see him slouching around in dark glasses and a pencil-thin mustache as the dissipated hotel and oil tycoon in the latter stages of the film. But his earlier depiction of the amoral, reckless, animal-like young ranch hand will not only excite his admirers to frenzy, it will make the most sedate onlooker understand why a James Dean cult ever came into existence."

In the *Saturday Review* (October 13, 1956), under a headline, "It's Dean, Dean, Dean," Hollis Alpert echoed the *Times* and the *Tribune*. "But it is the late James Dean, as Jett Rink, that the audiences will be watching—and there are many who will be watching him with fascination and love. For, as everyone knows, this young man who died in an auto smashup has caused a mass hysteria at least equal to that caused by Valentino."

The studio's big (forty-eight-page) press book for *Giant* side-stepped any mention of Jimmy's death. It concentrated on establishing links between his personality and the personality of the character he portrayed. It would have been impossible to learn that Jimmy was not alive and well (and living in Hollywood) from copy that spoke of him as "one of the most versatile actors of the Warner Bros. troupe" and "one of the screen's most dynamic and extraordinary performers."

The release of *Giant*, unlike that of *Rebel*, got the full "A" treatment: the best brains and a big budget. According to Richard Lederer, who was at that time a junior member of Warner Brothers' Advertising Department and who is now its head: "By the time *Giant* came out, James Dean had started to become a legend, a cult hero. And *East of Eden* is still—they sort of re-release it once every three years in Japan and it makes more money than a lot of our first-run pictures. In certain territories of the world, he's immortal, Jimmy Dean."

But he wasn't immortal enough at home to get an Oscar for either of his posthumous Academy Award nominations. In February 1956, he was nominated (the first time in the history of the Academy of Motion Picture Arts & Sciences that a nomination had gone to a dead actor) for Best Performance in *East of Eden*. In the New York *Times*, Sunday, March 4, 1956, five long and vehement letters disputed Oliver Evans' contention in the previous Sunday's paper that the nomination of a dead performer might be "a breach of good taste." But for all the support that Jimmy got, when Academy Award night came, Ernest Borgnine won the 1956 Best Performance Oscar for *Marty*. Jimmy was nominated again in 1957 for his work in *Giant*, but once more a living actor, Yul Brynner, for *The King and I*, walked away with the golden idol.

Jimmy's overseas admirers were more generous. He got several French film awards (including the highest, The

Crystal Star), an English Academy Award, a Belgian film award, a Finnish film journalists' award, and a number of Japanese trophies, the most important of which was the Million Pearl Award for the most popular foreign actor.

Back in Fairmount, Indiana, a James Dean Memorial Foundation was organized by a number of leading citizens, including Jimmy's Uncle Marcus, and several New York and Hollywood show-business people: acting teacher Sanford Meisner; director Coy Bronson; screenwriter Stewart Stern. In the summer of 1956, Bronson directed a brief benefit run of *Our Town* for the Foundation. The part of Joe Crowell was played by Marcus Winslow Jr., Jimmy's young cousin. For a time, there was a feeling on the Winslow farm that some of the Dean forensic fire—debating, auctioneering, acting—might be warming young Markie's blood. And for one performance, when a member of the regular cast got sick, the role of Mrs. Soames was played by Adeline Nall. She had flown in from New York, where, on leave from Fairmount High, she was making her own attempt to break through to Broadway.

Things seemed to be getting off to a fine start. But just three summers later, the Indianapolis *News* announced (almost gleefully): "JAMES DEAN THEATRE SCHOOL GOES BROKE. Shrine to Star Now a Furniture Store." In the story, Lewis Crist, the foundation's president, was quoted as saying, "Our dream is gone. We had something but it got away." Crist went on to explain the collapse as "a case of the big shots running over us hayseeds." And Reverend Xen Harvoy said he thought the foundation fiasco was brought on by "neurotic souls who came into town and attached themselves to the organization. Folks here," he went on to say, "aren't too happy about the situation."

The same article documented another development the townspeople weren't happy about: the beheading of the James Dean memorial column that had been set up just inside the entrance of Park Cemetery. Beneath the picture of the foundation-become-furniture-store was another showing the chimneylike brick column on which a twice life-size bronze head of Jimmy had been mounted. "In one brazen move," wrote the reporter, with unconscious irony, "they sawed off a bronze head in a cemetery memorial."

In the summer of 1957, ten months after the opening of *Giant*, Warner Brothers released a black and white movie called *The James Dean Story*. Produced by George W. George, directed by Robert Altman (who later did *M°A°S°H*), and written by Stewart Stern, the film consisted of clips, such as an unused *East of Eden* scene— Jimmy, sitting on the head of an iron bed talking to Dick Davalos, still photographs of Jimmy lovingly panned over and zoomed into, footage of various Fairmount landmarks, interviews with Indiana and Hollywood and New York people who had known Jimmy, a wire recording of Grandpa Charlie Dean's voice that Jimmy had once made, and some mood shots of trees, waves, and a dead seagull.

Warner Brothers didn't push the picture very hard. Fan mail for Jimmy at the studio had slipped considerably from its astounding 7,000-a-month peak. The press book was the smallest—only eight pages—that had ever been prepared for a James Dean picture. The opening wasn't in New York but at the Paramount Theatre in Marion, Indiana, where it was hoped that loyal local reaction might generate some good stories for the urban showings. But not much happened in Marion or anywhere else. Altman said later, demonstrating rare mastery of directorial double talk, "The people who came because of the title were disappointed; those who should have come were kept away by the title."

Certainly the title, *The James Dean Story,* wouldn't have kept anyone interested in Jimmy away from the picture. The trouble was deeper. Hunger for the Dean image had been very nearly satiated. Fan books such as *Movie Teen Illustrated* were beginning to print stories like: "Why Are Jimmy Dean Fans Switching to Tony Perkins?"

A few months after the release of *The James Dean Story,* a Truman Capote profile of Marlon Brando appeared in *The New Yorker.* Brando said "a friend" (Stewart Stern) had asked him to do the narration for the Dean documentary, and went on to explain that his motives for considering the job weren't based on any close association with the dead actor: "I hardly knew him. But he had an *idée fixe* about me. Whatever I did, he did. He was always trying to get close to me. He used to call me up . . . I'd listen to him talking to the answering service, asking for me, leaving messages. But I never spoke up. I never called him back . . .

"No, when I finally met Dean . . . it was at a party where he was throwing himself around, acting like a madman. So I spoke to him. I took him aside and asked him didn't he know he was sick. That he needed help . . . He listened to me. He knew he was sick. I gave him the name of an analyst and he went. And at least his *work* improved. Toward the end I think he was beginning to find his own way as an actor. But this glorifying of Dean is all wrong. That's why I believe the documentary could be important. To show he wasn't a hero; show what he really was—just a lost boy trying to find himself."

Twelve years later, in August 1969, *The New Yorker* interviewed the founder and president of America's most enduring Dean fan club, a fifty-seven-year-old widow named Therese J. Brandes. Although Mrs. Brandes shared the first five letters of her last name with Mr. Brando, she shared none of his feelings about her favorite movie star.

After Jimmy's death, she devoted her life to glorifying his memory. Until her own death a few years ago, anyone (with the possible exception of Mr. Brando) who wanted to talk about James Dean was welcome to drop in at her apartment on East Fifty-seventh Street. When she wasn't occupied with Dean visitors, she kept up a massive correspondence with Dean admirers—mostly teen-age pen pals—all over the world. She also wrote letters to network TV executives to make sure that their schedules included frequent re-runs of James Dean films.

Each year, on Jimmy's birthday, and on his deathday, she had flowers put on his grave. Jimmy's uncle, Marcus Winslow, handled this assignment for her and even took photographs of the flowers so that club members back in New York could see what they were getting for their contributions. Each year, too, using the "In Memoriam" column in the *Daily News,* she collected money for various charities in Jimmy's name.

"If you're thinking that James Dean is forgotten," said Mrs. Brandes, "you're absolutely wrong. He's not. Sometimes on television these days there'll be a band—today's new type of band—and they'll have a big poster of James Dean, and they're playing this modern music. The young people know about James Dean. And then another time somebody will be talking—like a discussion program, discussing a movie—and the name of James Dean comes up. So James Dean is not forgotten. And with me and the other members of the club, he'll never be forgotten, because we're always talking about him. I always tell people that James Dean will be alive until I die."

Even longer. The James Dean myth has now survived Mrs. Brandes and will probably last as long as our culture has any use for the Icarian archetype, the innocent youth who dies a tragic death before he can fail either himself or us. After our culture collapses, it seems likely that the god images we chiseled into stone will have a better chance of being dug up than those we fixed on film. But such speculation may be inappropriately cosmic. Richard Lederer, with pragmatic perspective gained from years in a Hollywood star factory, probably puts it best: "In certain territories of the world he's immortal, Jimmy Dean."

AN ASTROLOGICAL READING *by John Beck*

James Dean
February 8, 1931
2:00 A.M. CST
Marion, Indiana 41°N, 86°W

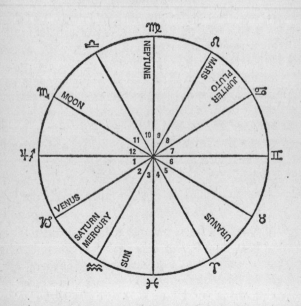

A Sagittarius ascendant made James Dean seem to be forever seeking new dimensions in which to express himself. His brand of freedom required people, but, at the same time, kept him one step removed from them. His mind and emotions were free-ranging, and bluntly assertive in the face of any limitation. He had a certain awkward charm and was restless without being indecisive. He was likely to act decisively in one way, and then just as decisively in another, because he tried to see himself in others' eyes and didn't dare appear to fall short of his own idealistic standards.

James Dean's sun was in Aquarius. Aquarians tend to be idealistic and unconventional by definition. They seek freedom for themselves and for humanity. This makes them original, creative, artistic, and unpredictable. They are attractive and friendly, but their love of mankind spreads their feelings thinly. They are apt to get involved in causes with such passion that they can become rebellious and even perverse in pursuit of their goals. The same spirit that prompts originality and independence in Aquarians can also make them dogmatic and authoritarian—they see this intensity as progressive and farsighted even if they resort to dictatorial means to overcome a dictatorship.

The Aquarian mind is both intuitive and intelligent and works in a scientific way to sort out experiences even before others have become aware of them. Aquarians want to be true to a cause or to a loved one, but their involvement can become dispassionate. They are apt to lose sight of immediate goals or to break the heart of a lover in pursuit of something on a grander scale. At their worst, Aquarians can be eccentric, fanatical, and tactless. They are at their best when their progressive attitudes and active minds can be utilized—especially in group endeavors. They do well with science, modern communication (radio, TV, photography, movies, etc.), and community rights. A job that would allow an experimental approach to correcting injustice and that used communications as a tool would be ideal.

Having the sun in the third house means that intimate exchange should have been the integrating element in James Dean's life. However, because of other influences on the sun, his associations with relatives or close friends brought him more pain than pleasure. Those who were close to him should have made him cheerful and open. Instead, they were a source of trouble and misunderstanding. Nevertheless, as a seeker of knowledge, he wanted to absorb what he could from those who were his intimates, and he wanted to show others what he learned. He was a communicator by nature, in both word and action, so he was always seeking some ultimate means of expressing the difficult message inside him.

The ascendant and the sun are just two of the elements in a complete horoscope. The influence of each of these is altered by other things in the chart. When two elements in a horoscope are at a major angle to each other, they are said to be aspected. Major angles are 0°, 30°, 60°, 90°, 120°, 150°, and 180°. Also considered are 45° and 135°, but they are not as important. Aspects modify the impact of the two planets which form the angle. Some aspects cause forces to pull together and others make them work against one another. Elements in a chart are often aspected into a whole package of influence. This is exactly what happens in the case of James Dean. His chart can be divided into two distinct packages: one involving the ascendant; the other involving the sun. The first package looks like this:

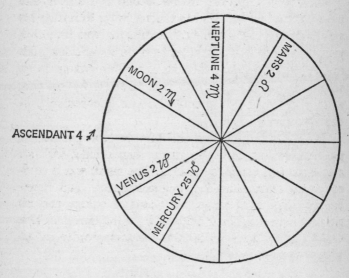

The first package is set off by Mars in opposition with (172 to 188 degrees from) Mercury. Mars in Leo in the eighth house gave James Dean tremendous amounts of energy that he directed toward the possessions and feelings of others. Sensual or psychic things appealed to him and he pursued them with force. He also got help from others in the way of money or jobs. His creative energy was limitless and he sought exciting, powerful, and dangerous ways to use it. He was physically strong (like lightning, not like a mountain), very active, and prone to accidents. His passions were electric and attracted women as well as lucky breaks. Many people were enchanted by his strength, but many others were overwhelmed by it.

Mercury in Capricorn in the second house gave him the ability to use his mind in rational ways to further his ambitions and make money. His thinking was inventive, yet he wanted details in order to understand things. His mind was practical and cautious as well as curious. In essence, he protected his own best interests by knowing what was going on around him and proceeding prudently with that knowledge.

The opposition of Mars and Mercury brought his impulsive, reckless, magnetic energy into conflict with his ambitious and cautious thinking. The result was a tendency to overexhaustion, pugnaciousness, and unreliability. His mind feared his bursts of energy and his passions resented being held back by his thoughts. This conflict could have made him manic-depressive at extreme moments in his life.

The Mars-Mercury tension is increased by the moon, which is in square with (82 to 98 degrees from) both planets. The moon in Scorpio in the eleventh house made James Dean want to have associates rather than close friends. Like the Aquarius sun, it signals an attraction for groups in which he could work toward some idealistic goal without getting personally entangled. In group endeavors, he usually had some objective of his own that he was trying to satisfy independent of the stated goal of the project. Nevertheless, he pursued the common end with emotional commitment. The moon in Scorpio made him feel as if he were facing the world's problems alone. It also made him insist upon his own courage. But he struggled so hard to be strong that overintensity often forced the result he least intended. He masked his loneliness with a tough surface and at times was angry, vengeful, and insistent upon his own terms. He was a sensual, but with sex, as with all other emotions, he remained erratic and impersonal.

In square to Mercury, the moon made James Dean quick to react, but overly quick to change his mind. It also made him nervous and restless. The moon in square with Mars added to his impulsiveness by placing the deep moods of the moon in conflict with the raw force of Mars. It also tended to make him intolerant and indiscreet.

The way these three planets are aspected forms what is called a T-square. With this kind of pattern, the planet on the stem of the T often gives the tension a direction. In this case, the conflict between energy and thought sought an outlet through group endeavors. Such projects gave James Dean a chance to focus his self-assurance and self-doubt, to intuitively express his experiences to the world. The impersonality of an organized group kept him safe from his outbursts of passion, and the objectives of the group satisfied his ambition. Group effort made better use of the conflicts inside him than any other form of endeavor.

Venus alters the effect of this T-square since it is in difficult aspect with Mars and easy aspect with the moon.

Venus in Capricorn in the first house gave James Dean good looks and made him attractive. It also added an artistic side to his charm. He sought social amusement and enjoyed being the center of social attention. However, his love attachments were cautious to the point of being cynical. He held back his affections in order to find out what he would get in return. If he did risk loving, he expected response selfishly. In relations with people in higher positions, his affection-seeking brought him success.

In quincunx with Mars, Venus' charm and affection-seeking brought him great discontent. They underlined the erotic impulses of Mars in the eighth house by making him pour excessive emotion into relationships that could not possibly give him the response he wanted. This must have left him unsatisfied and unhappy, and he may even have resented the breaks he got from people above him.

In sextile with the moon, Venus added to his creativity and artistic talent, and allowed him to be friendly, even affectionate in his group work. As long as he didn't have to get too personally involved, his emotions would be somewhat less stormy and his surface charm could dominate.

Neptune also has an impact on the T-square. Neptune in Virgo in the tenth house gave James Dean a career that was inspired and artistic. He was intuitive to the point of being psychic, and had great feeling for small animals, flowers, and hidden motivations in people. He was probably critical of religion and psychism since his intuition was primarily oriented toward the world. His sixth sense made him romantic and idealistic about his role in life, and overly conscious of prestige. It also gave him the power to translate his own experiences (which otherwise he kept hidden) into instructional forms. By looking back to the sun in the third house, it can be seen that intuition was one of the integrating forces in his life, and gave him the chance to make a career out of his ability.

In sextile with the moon, Neptune linked James Dean's group involvement with his life work in a compatible way. It added creative potential which made him more able to express his intuitions and hidden experiences artistically. It also provided an easy means of directing the insecurity of the moon's influence into a viable outlet.

Neptune is in trine with (112 to 128 degrees from) Venus. This most beneficial of aspects combined his attractiveness and his practical use of feelings with his career. It promised him successful means of expressing his ideals and feelings through art, and music should have been soothing to him if he pursued it.

Neptune is also in semi-sextile with (28 to 34 degrees from) Mars. This means that when James Dean directed his energies into sensitive and artistic projects the mental and emotional confusion which he suffered would be even further aggravated. It gave him the potential to project himself so far into a role that he could fall into escapism and self-deception.

The ascendant is also part of this package of planets and it has an influence on the T-square. In trine with

Mars, the ascendant made his explosive outbursts appear to be part of his free-spirited hunger for understanding. People could explain his need to knock down barriers and his lust for danger as steps toward a new kind of freedom, something more idealistic and pure than they could grasp.

In semi-sextile with Venus, the ascendant put his quest in the way of any satisfaction he might have known from love. Instead, he found that his need for no restraints brought him disharmony and disappointment.

In square with Neptune, the ascendant made a link between James Dean's personality and his career. This difficult aspect made his outward appearance conflict with the role he aspired to, and caused him to become all but neurotic in his self-deception.

To sum up this first package of planetary influence: James Dean had strong inner conflicts between his cautious, ambitious thoughts and his impulsive, power-seeking energy. This conflict sought an outlet through emotions applied to group goals which he used to satisfy his own masqueraded needs for security. He was able to blend personal charm, artistic ability, and intuition into his group involvement, and out of these he molded a career. His work was most satisfying to him if he thought it served some humanistic ideal while at the same time giving him a role into which to project himself. His personality was attractive, even magnetic, but he could not allow others to get close enough to touch him. Those who knew him saw him as always wanting some new freedom, as forever pushing beyond the world he knew. He had the strength, talent, and ambition to create new worlds, but he could also set out recklessly in pursuit of goals which even he could not envision.

The second package of influence looks like this:

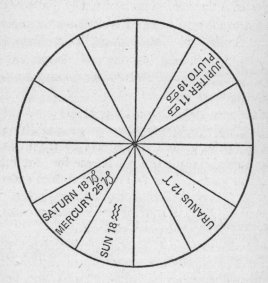

The second package of planets in James Dean's horoscope is marked by an opposition between the eighth and second houses. In the eighth house, Pluto and Jupiter are in conjunction (within 8 degrees) and both planets are in Cancer. These are both in opposition with Saturn, and Pluto is also in opposition with Mercury. Pluto is the ruler of the eighth house so it is especially strong there. It is the planet of regeneration, which influences anything to do with death and rebirth, ranging from legacies (which see money change hands and start anew), to sex (which sees old emotions discharged and new feelings begun), to abrupt changes in lifestyle, to death itself. Pluto moves through the signs so slowly that it tends to have a generational effect. In Cancer it causes people to experience their old notions of family, protection, and nourishment being destroyed while new concepts take over. In the eighth, Pluto brought James Dean violent upheavals. He probably experienced abrupt and unexpected partings from members of his family, and he was destined for a violent death.

Jupiter in the eighth house brought him good luck from close relations with others. Many people probably passed things on to him, either in the form of money or positions. Jupiter here also made death a release for him, bringing with it the sense that he was expanding into a new life. Jupiter in Cancer indicates that his benefactors would be protective. He would also try to be protective in a way that bound people to him restrictively.

The conjunction of Pluto and Jupiter shows that he would break suddenly from those who cared for him and from those for whom he cared. This pattern probably started with separations in his family and carried over to later loves. In each pile of emotional ashes he found the spirit to go on to greater achievements. These painful experiences pushed him to cling to things rather than people, and it may also have led him to feel that keeping his distance was the only way to protect others from himself.

Saturn in Capricorn in the second house made James Dean sensible and prudent about money, property, and his own feelings. It also added to his caution and ambition. Saturn is the ruler of Capricorn and is so strong there that it could turn his caution inward toward selfish ends. Mercury in conjunction with this adds mental impact that made him want to be coolly in charge of everything around him—money, ideas, emotions, even people. This conjunction also led him to depressive thinking since it provided a practical side to his character that was impossible to fulfill.

The opposition between the eighth and second houses put James Dean's emotional endings and beginnings in conflict with his strong needs for security and planning. Jupiter in opposition with Saturn caused him losses and frustration since he could not accept his own limitations. Saturn in opposition with Pluto built these frustrations into obsessions that resulted in periodic blow-ups and acts of violence. And Mercury in opposition with Pluto added disturbing thoughts which led to explosive moods. As long as he was able to control his feelings, James Dean was likely to find social and financial success. Even his losses were bound to bring him greater success. However, in order to maintain this control, he had to blow off so much tension that, in time, these explosions must have shattered his desire to control at all.

Uranus forms a T-square with this opposition. Uranus in Aries in the fifth house made him even more impulsive and independent. Because Uranus is awkwardly placed in the chart, these tendencies were expressed in bluntness, irritability, and abrupt changefulness, all of which made life disruptive and unpleasant for him and for those around him. Uranus also made his mind active and fertile (approaching genius level). It added to his strength of will and heightened his utopian views. Nevertheless, these positive traits were pursued so impulsively and with such jolting force that they tended to bring him trouble, especially with love affairs and recklessness. When restrained or focused, Uranus made him brilliant; when not, it pushed him to extremes.

The square between Saturn and Uranus put very severe limits on his fiery creative impulses. It tended to make him egotistical on one side and potentially cruel on the other. The square between Jupiter and Uranus combined good luck and a sense of personal growth with his recklessness, and this tended to make him antisocial in dramatic ways. He wouldn't just stay away from people, he would get intensely involved with them so that he could then run off and do something extravagant *without* them. The square between Uranus and Pluto made him exceptionally creative and violently destructive at the same time.

As with the T-square in the first package, the tension between extreme caution and uncontrollable passion was directed through the stem of this T. He displayed creativity and brilliance which was directed for the betterment of humanity, but this was offset by his tendency to change quickly from one thing to the next, to take excessive risks, and to disrupt lives around him. He probably played biting intellectual games which were designed both to display his idealistic views and keep people at a distance.

The sun influences this T-square, since it is in easy aspect with Uranus and in difficult aspect with Saturn and Jupiter. The sun in sextile with Uranus gave James Dean one place to focus his creative forcefulness. He was able to direct his risk-taking intelligence into communication, and to satisfy some of his desires to express himself publicly. His intentions in this area were good. His motivations always had a cool sort of kindness and a benevolent spirit behind them, even when he was most hurtful to himself or to others.

The sun in semi-sextile with Saturn, however, tended to make it more difficult for him to feel that his inner spirit could live up to his ambitions, or overcome his limitations.

The sun in quincunx with Jupiter reduced the good luck that Jupiter brought him by giving him a false sense of superiority which, of course, made it harder for him to achieve his goals.

To sum up this second package of planetary influences: the creative, progressive, independence-seeking motives of James Dean's sun gained extra ability and energy, and gave him an even greater willingness to risk everything he had to achieve his purposes. His frustrations distorted his idealistic principles and made him selfish in his actions. He had outstanding ability to communicate with people, but this was not enough; he sought ever more challenging frontiers and greater risks. This drive estranged him from people and added to his frustrations. Loves and risks were torrid but short-lived. He wanted to be independent and he pushed others to be independent of him, but the world inside him was in conflict with his inability to control. What he could do was undeniably brilliant, but he was forced into extreme roles to accomplish success, and these roles left success behind him in ashes.

There are two places where the first package of planets and the second meet. The first is Mercury which is the only planet that is involved in both packages. The one unifying element in his life was his mental caution, his ambition, and his calculating watchfulness of others. The second link is the tension between the second and eighth houses which sets off both packages of influence. The second house brought James Dean success through hard work, but he had to pretend to be the toughest, most independent person in the world to achieve it. And underlying this veneer was much kindness and creativity mixed with self-doubt and emotional pain.

Opposed to this hard-earned success, the eighth house gave James Dean explosive energy that brought him many easy triumphs. But success was short-lived and followed by painful personal and professional ruptures. It was only a matter of time until one burst of energy or another would be more than he could control. No worldly conquest could quench his thirst to know more. Nobody could answer the unanswerable questions he had about his own perplexing nature. No role could take him out of his own skin, no matter how far he threw himself into it.

BIBLIOGRAPHICAL NOTE

People frequently steal James Dean material. Photographs and articles and reviews have disappeared from Lincoln Center's Library of the Performing Arts, from the Film Library of The Museum of Modern Art, from the Library of The Academy of Motion Picture Arts and Sciences. Warner Brothers' files have been raided, too.

This means that getting on James Dean's trail is no ordinary scholarly task. You do not report to the library every morning and retreat to your carrel. You go out and forage for interviews, books, newspapers, magazines, publicity releases, movie scripts, plays, letters, memos, photographs, records, tapes. If you're lucky you run into one or more people who have a private James Dean hoard, and who like you well enough to let you use it. By now I have a roomful of James Dean material, bought, borrowed, but not, in spite of terrible temptation at various moments, stolen.

In the years immediately following Dean's death—1956, 1957, 1958, 1959—there was an avalanche of newspaper and magazine interest in his life and in his films. Articles and pictures appeared in dailies and weeklies across the country and in *Collier's, Commentary, Coronet, Cosmopolitan, Esquire, Evergreen Review, Life, Look, Modern Screen, Motion Picture, Movieland, Movie Life, Movie Mirror, Movie Stars Parade,* the *New Republic, Newsweek, Photoplay, Popular Photography, Redbook, The Reporter, Saturday Review, Sight and Sound, Seventeen, Screen Stars, Screen Stories, Time, Theatre Arts, Vogue.* There were, in addition, dozens of special albums, annuals, and pieces in smaller magazines. Publications in England, France, Germany, Italy, and Japan, also printed up a James Dean storm.

Particularly valuable in my search have been the books of the two men, who, in my opinion, most seriously sought James Dean before me: William Bast's enthusiastic, insightful, 1956 memoir-biography, *James Dean* (Ballantine Books), and Robert Wayne Tysl's heroic 670-page doctoral thesis: *Continuity and Evolution in a Public Symbol: An Investigation into the Creation and Communication of the James Dean Image in Mid-Century America* (1965).

INDEX